FLY FISHING
SOUTHERN CALIFORNIA'S
LAKES & STREAMS

TO JAY.

ENJOY OUR LOCAL Angling!

FLY FISHING SOUTHERN CALIFORNIA'S LAKES & STREAMS

By Richard Alden Bean

Aguabonita Books

FOR INFORMATION WRITE:
Aguabonita Books
PO Box 8535
Truckee, CA 96162

Text Copyright ©2000 by Richard Alden Bean
Maps Copyright ©2000 Aguabonita Books

PHOTOGRAPHY CREDITS: All text and cover photography Copyright © 2000 by Richard Alden Bean unless otherwise noted.
Front Cover photograph Copyright © 2000 by John E. Nordstrand
Photograph on page 52 Copyright © 2000 Jim Matthews

Maps by Litton Design, San Francisco

Library of Congress Catalog Card Number:

ISBN 0-9652566-1-8

Printed in Hong Kong

First Edition
M 10 9 8 7 6 5 4 3 2 1

This edition produced for Aguabonita Books by:

Barich Books
870 Market Street, Suite 690
San Francisco, CA 94102

This book is for my sons, Eric and John, who caught my bad habit of fishing. It is especially dedicated to my youngest boy, Dick, 1963–1998. He now fishes in other waters.

TABLE OF CONTENTS

WHY SOUTHERN CALIFORNIA?

AUTHOR: "I'M GOING TO WRITE A FLY-FISHING GUIDE to Southern California."

Fly-fishing friend: "Why?"

Don't laugh. It's an attitude that all too often limits the conversation when anglers in the southern half of the state talk fly fishing. In casual, over-the-counter conversations at the local fly shop, or in group discussions during club meetings, most (if not all) of the talk is about places other than Southern California. If it isn't the sparkling streams of the eastern Sierra or the great rivers of Northern California, then it's the quality waters in Montana, Idaho, Utah, New Mexico, Baja, Florida, or...well, you get the idea.

Anywhere but here. A decade ago, I abruptly quit a local fly-fishing club when the president got up in front of the audience and stated: "I only fish for trout, I only fish dry flies, and I only fish on the _____ River." The water, which shall remain nameless, is not in California. It is a quality stream, but it hardly merits the exclusive label this guy put on it. In recent years, I've seen more than one letter in fishing magazines lamenting the crowded conditions on this hallowed water, with anglers standing shoulder to shoulder, and the shocking decline in stream manners that has accompanied the crowding.

I wouldn't have been quite as irritated when our "expert" announced his narrow view of fly fishing, except the group was laced with new members. Most of them were beginners who soaked up every word of the older, and presumably wiser, angler. I noted soon afterward that they began to adopt the same snobbish attitude. I found myself defending the local streams and lakes in a number of situations and noticed, with sour amusement, that Mr.-I.-Only-Fish had created several disciples. That's when I walked.

I don't believe that dry-fly fishing is the only way to catch a trout or any other fish. I know for a fact that if you confine your angling efforts and enjoyment to the various salmonids, you are missing some of the best fly fishing of all. This is particularly true in Southern California, where the quality of the angling for species other than trout is as good as or better than it is almost anywhere else. This guide will cover in detail fly-fishing opportunities for both trout and other species in the Southern California area—without apology, and without elitist nonsense.

Truth to tell, Southern California isn't the garden spot of fly fishing. Southern California is a desert. Even the limited strip of green along the coastal mountains only just manages to rise above that designation, and even this area is subject to rainfall patterns that would constitute drought in most other parts of the country. Its higher elevations are forested, but winters never are anything like they are in the north. The ski areas often

Southern California's mountain lakes offer both trout and bass angling, plus beautiful scenery. Here, the author's wife, Barbara, wades the shallows of Grout Bay at Big Bear Lake.

survive on man-made snow. That's an interesting use of a precious resource, since most of the mountain ranges have been tapped for every drop of liquid that runs downhill.

Southern California is too crowded with people, freeways, strip malls, and all the other junk and clutter of civilization, gets too little rain, and exists primarily on water "borrowed" from underground aquifers or removed from other parts of the state. A few years ago, I even read of a plan to build a pipeline to Alaska to ensure enough fresh water to continue development well into the twenty-second century!

This all sounds awfully gloomy. On the other hand, while the demand for drinking water and electrical power for the multitudes has altered or destroyed a number of waters, some excellent fishing opportunities remain, and more than a few stillwater fisheries actually have been created that never existed before, some of them worthy of serious attention.

One of the hard things about writing a fishing guide is that, sure as shootin', the day after it shows up on bookshelves, some guy will be writing a letter wanting to know why I ignored his favorite fishing spot. Even worse, I expect some to be put out that I revealed their "secret" stream or pond. In country as crowded as Southern California, there are few—if any—secret fishing hideaways. That doesn't mean I've found each and every fishery of interest, though. What I've tried to do is give readers a good start on locating the best fishing. And this guide is not and never can be complete. Things change too quickly in Southern California.

Actually, however, I've had to limit the scope of this book because of the wide variety of excellent fly fishing to be found in the lower half of the Golden State. I've excluded the eastern Sierra altogether. It deserves a guidebook of its own. Saltwater fly-fishing opportunities, which abound in Southern California, deserve another guidebook, as well.

What is left? This book covers the area south of the Tehachapi Mountain range. Included are freshwater angling opportunities in Ventura, Los Angeles, Orange, San Bernardino, Riverside, San Diego, and Imperial Counties. A few waters to the north of the Tehachapis are of such quality and are so close to most of the anglers in Southern California, however, that they are also covered. So is angling in the reservoirs and tailrace fisheries along the stretch of the Colorado River that forms the border between California and Arizona.

By my rough count, this guide covers an area with nearly fifty free-flowing streams or creeks that contain either wild trout, planted trout, or both. A surprising number have brown trout. Only the Kern River—and the wide sweep of the Colorado—are really big enough to merit the term "river," but a fair number are big enough to drown you if you make a misstep. At the time of this writing, three are recognized by the Department of Fish and Game as Wild Trout waters, and two more are designated as streams in the Catch-And-Release Program.

Strap-on electronic fish-finders should not be considered luxuries, as they allow float-tubing anglers to quickly locate fish-holding structure.

Many of the other streams are brooks or trickles that support wild fish, but don't expect these little treasures to yield their secrets easily. In most, the resident fish are small, and conditions often are marginal. The steep canyons down which these streams tumble raise tiny trout and big rattlesnakes. More often than not, they are not readily accessible without a hike. Virtually all are on National Forest or Bureau of Land Management lands, and for a fair number, access routes are controlled by various water companies and hydropower interests. Locked gates are the rule, and on some, a rugged four-wheel-drive vehicle is necessary to reach streamside.

Some of the angling these streams provide is of real quality. Quality fishing doesn't always require big fish. I've fished streams in Southern California where a trophy-sized trout would reach the 8-inch mark if you pulled hard on its nose and tail. A very few of these waters will allow a day of fishing where the average trout runs 8 to 9 inches, with a 12-inch fish something to brag about. My best trout from Deep Creek was an honest 17 inches, and Don Stehsel, head of the Fisheries Resource Volunteer Corps, a group of concerned anglers who work with the California Department of Fish and Game and the Forest Service to maintain and improve Southern California's trout streams, has caught and released a number of wild brown trout there which went over the 20-inch mark. This, however, is the exception.

As for stillwater fly fishing for trout, the opportunities are limited to put-and-take action, except for a few waters that allow holdover fish to prosper. If you don't mind the crowds, a few lakes offer fishing for awesome stocked trout. I've seen anglers hooked up to brood-stock rainbows weighing over 20 pounds, and hefty, healthy fish from the Whitewater Hatchery and others are stocked in a number of lakes. The Southland is unique in that most of the trout fishing in lakes comes not in the spring, but in fall, and runs through the winter months as low-altitude waters cool enough to support trout. This isn't all bad, because it offers a resource to the fly angler just as the trout season is closing up north. A number of the streams remain accessible, and in fact have better fishing in the winter than in summer's heat.

Southern California also has some of the best bass fishing in the world. A few years ago, angling writer Matt Vincent prepared a listing for *Bassmaster* magazine of the 25 largest bass ever taken by any method. Discounting George Perry's 1932 record of 22 pounds, 6 ounces caught in Georgia, and three others, all of the remaining 21 giant bass on the list were caught in California. Even better, 20 of them came from Southern California lakes, and the twenty-fifth on the list came from Lake Isabella, one of the lakes north of the Tehachapis that will be covered in this guide.

The number of lakes is large enough to give you something to do on a different lake each weekend of the year—and then some. A quick count of Southern California waters reveals no less than 50 lakes that can be fished with flies. As with the streams, some are jewels, some are paste. The quality still waters get detailed treatments in this book, and a few of the others are of interest, too.

In Chapter 5, and again in Chapter 7, you'll get information on some of the finest bass-fishing waters to be found anywhere. All are within a couple of hours' drive of Los Angeles, and a number offer more than just the potential to land a record fish on any cast, representing beautiful places that serve as scenic escapes from the freeways and smog.

Along with truly exceptional bass fishing, Southern California has plenty of fishing for the misnamed "lesser" species. Bluegills, crappies, and redear sunfish provide countless hours of enjoyment for anglers of all ages if they ain't too snobbish to love these handsome creatures. Panfish are just plain fun on fly tackle, and they are found everywhere. In a sophisticated age when many anglers have released every fish they've ever caught, panfish that actually wind up in a pan are a special treat. A few waters include amazing populations, and some have strains that produce bluegills and redears as big as dinner plates. I'll cover these species, as well as the others, in these chapters.

Our other major freshwater fish is the striped bass. Introduced to Southern California waters by a series of missteps and bad judgments, striped bass are present in at least five Southern California waters and probably will show up in others. Prolific and hardy, striped bass not only offer a lot of fishing action, but as with the panfishes, they likewise can form the basis of a gourmet meal for anglers who wouldn't think of killing a trout for the table. They taste better than trout, too.

Each chapter gives the reader a quick overview of the waters contained in the portion of Southern California being covered, then discusses them in greater detail, beginning with the best waters, followed by the good, and ending with those of lesser potential. Access routes and trail notes are given for streams. For lakes, all the pertinent information on entrance, boat rental and/or launch fees, marinas, and services is listed. Suggestions for camping or lodging, guides, and a host of other information is included. (Fees reflect 1999 prices.) Maps showing the locations of the best waters accompany each chapter. There's also an Appendix listing of other resources that will interest the fly fisher.

Chapter 9 covers a few waters that don't fit the pattern of those discussed in earlier chapters. Some of these offbeat fly-fishing opportunities will interest avid anglers, others will probably repel them. That's OK. These waters aren't for everyone.

The next time you get a sudden desire to go fishing, rather than planning a trip to some remote destination, grab this guide and thumb through the possibilities in Southern California. The Southland offers the fly angler year-around fishing for many freshwater fish.

CHAPTER ONE

THE NORTH OF THE SOUTH

VENTURA AND SANTA BARBARA COUNTIES, LYING TO the north of the most densely populated portions of the Los Angeles basin, have a mix of excellent angling for largemouth bass, stripers, and hatchery trout in a number of large reservoirs. There also are streams, some holding southern steelhead.

Because it is located just to the north of Los Angeles County, it would seem at first glance that Ventura County would be nothing more than an extension of the urban sprawl of Los Angeles. It is true that the lower quarter, along Highways 101 and 126, has low-density cities and towns like Oxnard and Simi Valley, but the vast majority of the county is locked up inside the Los Padres National Forest.

Encompassing almost two million acres, Los Padres is the third largest national forest in California. It occupies a major portion of the Pacific coastal mountain ranges and extends for about 220 miles, from the west boundary of Los Angeles County to mid-Monterey County on the north. The forest is the key to the trout streams. It is largely roadless, and in Ventura, the Sespe Condor Sanctuary, and the Sespe and Chumash Wilderness Areas, prohibit most vehicular access.

Santa Barbara County contains a continuation of the Los Padres National Forest. Much of the coast of Santa Barbara County faces almost directly south, giving some a false sense of where the compass points are. The main population centers of Santa Barbara, Lompoc and Santa Maria, all are as near to the coast as the national forest and sprawling Vandenberg Air Force Base will allow, while the interior mountain ranges are largely road-free.

These coastal mountain ranges are dryer than you might suspect. Like much of Southern California, they get their water in a winter rush of rain and sometimes snow, but may go for months during the summer and fall without any rain at all. The streams are seasonal and many get too low to fish by mid-summer, even though trout survive in the larger pools and around natural springs and tiny feeder creeks that flow all year. Despite this unfavorable environment, the waters here are incredibly rich.

In addition to the lakes and streams within these counties, I've added one lake that is actually in Los Angeles County. Castaic Lake is a California Aqueduct reservoir that lies just to the east of the Ventura–Los Angeles County line. As a bass and striper fishery, it doesn't quite fit in the chapter on mountain lakes, and it has more in common with the other lakes in this chapter than with waters elsewhere.

CASTAIC LAKE

SPECIES: Florida-strain largemouth bass, striped bass, hatchery trout, plus the possible introduction of Florida-strain bluegills soon.

Sespe Creek is typical of Southern California streams: smallish fish, arid watersheds.

BEST TIME: The fall through the spring.
FLIES: For bass, shad streamers and crayfish patterns. Stripers key on planted trout and shad. Try big streamers, such as Lefty's Deceivers or Blanton's Sar-Mul-Macs in rainbow-trout colors.
FLOAT TUBES: Yes, but only in the lower lake. A launch fee is charged.
LOCATION: 45 miles north of Los Angeles on Interstate 5 Turn east off Interstate 5 in Castaic, then follow Lake Hughes Road to the dam.

If there are bass anglers in California who haven't heard of Castaic Lake, they probably have been living in caves for the last ten years or so. I realize this lake may not be too familiar to fly anglers who tend to think about trout, but this is a bass water that needs more attention from fly fishers who are interested in trophy largemouth bass, an attraction that Castaic shares with Lake Casitas, also in this chapter. From the mid-1980s to the early 1990s, Castaic probably got more press in local and national media than any other lake in the state. The reason was simple: big bass and lots of them. Of the 25 largest bass of all time listed in Bart Crabb's *Quest For the World Record Bass* (disregarding Paul Duclos's huge estimated 24-pound bass caught in Northern California on March 1, 1997, the subject of much controversy), 7 were caught at Castaic.

Castaic is or was one of the finest largemouth bass fisheries in the world. The largest properly recorded largemouth bass in modern times, a monster just a hair over 22 pounds caught and released by trophy specialist Bob Crupi in 1991, was a Castaic bass, and so was the recognized California state record fish, a 21-pound, 12-ounce fish also taken in 1991 by Mike Aurjo. If you examine the line-class records in the 1997 International Game Fish Association book, you find that Castaic accounts for 6 of the 7 records.

A unique set of factors created Castaic. It is not a natural lake. Like nearly all Southern California waters, Castaic is a reservoir. It is part of the California Water Project, a system of canals, reservoirs and pumping stations that bring water to Southern California from the northern half of the state. Castaic, opened in 1971, is the last reservoir on the western branch of the California Aqueduct. In addition to storing water, Castaic also produces electrical power from a powerhouse just north of the lake.

There actually are two lakes at Castaic. The main lake, a big, 2,235-acre body of water, is shaped like a V. It has a total of 29 miles of shoreline. The western or ski arm of the lake gets traffic from personal watercraft and water skiers, while the fish arm on the east has areas with 5-mile-per-hour speed limits for anglers. Florida-strain and hybrid largemouth bass provide the prime fishery there, having been stocked at the time the lake was being filled. In recent years, striped bass have made their way through the aqueduct system into nearly all the Water Project reservoirs, and Castaic is no exception. The striper population there is on the rise, and this worries a lot of bass anglers and some biologists.

Although some of Southern California's streams run through brush-filled canyons, others (like the Sespe above) have relatively open channels that usually allow plenty of room for casting.

Frankly, I take the opposite view. As a fly angler, I like diversity. A stream with both brown and rainbow trout (or goldens, or brookies) is of more interest to me than a monoculture habitat, no matter how scenic or unspoiled it is. Likewise, a lake that offers several species of fish to catch always is more fun. Organized bass anglers, on the other hand, those who compete in tournaments, are a major force in Southern California, and they don't like striped bass.

The striped bass fishery at Castaic has grown from a sometime thing to a full-blown melee when rainbow trout are stocked in the lake. Striper "boils" of large fish chasing trout are easy to see, and the stocked fish lure the stripers into densities that make them easy to catch. A large streamer fly or pencil popper, properly presented, could be the trigger that brings a strike from ten or more pounds of truly wild fish.

Castaic is known as a "structure" lake, where the biggest bass are normally caught by anglers who fish primary points and deep features. Bass guide Gary Harrison says he likes to fish the methods and tactics that have produced results in the past because they still work, but also notes that it is possible that some of the very largest bass have switched from being structure-oriented to mimicking the behavior of the striped bass. Harrison believes that instead of hanging around rocks or other deep features, they have taken up an open-water existence, following the schools of shad and trout with the stripers. So does Troy Folkestad. A full-time fishing guide and tournament angler,

Folkestad comes from a fishing family. His father, Mike Folkestad, is a well-known bass pro.

"I caught 23 bass over 8 pounds at Castaic last year—that's by far the best season I've had in 26 years of bass fishing," noted Folkestad. "That's not counting the big fish my clients have caught. That's just me." He thinks you still can catch fish on structure, but they aren't the biggest fish, and there are not as many there.

Although the lake is part of the California Aqueduct system, it is operated by the Los Angeles County Parks and Recreation Department. Below the main, V-shaped lake, which was formed in the junction of two canyons, sits what is often called "Castaic Lagoon," which is just 3 miles around and 197 surface acres and also has a good population of largemouth bass, in addition to bluegills, crappies, catfish, and stocked trout. Some of the larger bass in recent years have come from here, and it is a popular spot with many anglers. The lower lake also allows fishing from the shore twenty-four hours a day.

Castaic is open year round except for Christmas Day. Entry fees are $6.00 per day per car, except on weekdays from November to February, when no fee is charged. Boat launching is $6.00. There are senior citizen and annual fee passes available.

Call the lake office at (661) 257-4050 for a list of options or for a fishing report. There is camping both at the lake and in nearby private camps. Food, lodging, and other services can be found in close proximity. For vacationing anglers, Magic Mountain Park is only 7 miles away. Sources for up-to-date fishing information include the marina, (661) 257-2049, and the Mobile Mini-Mart, (661) 257-3717.

LAKE PIRU

SPECIES: Northern-strain largemouth bass, hatchery trout, bluegills.
BEST TIME: The winter and spring, but good year-round.
FLIES: Shad imitations, Clouser Deep Minnows, Woolly Buggers. Northern-strain bass delight in hitting poppers.
FLOAT TUBES: Yes, but presently with some restrictions. See below.
LOCATION: 50 miles northwest of Los Angeles. Take Interstate 5 north to Castaic Junction, then west on Highway 126 to Piru, turn north, and follow the signs.

Located at the eastern end of Ventura County, Lake Piru isn't large, as Southern California reservoirs go. Maximum surface acreage peaks at around 1,200, and during the winter drawdown, it can shrink to as little as 750 acres, but Piru is very big in another way. When you start asking experienced bass anglers from the Los Angeles basin about their favorite lakes, Piru's name comes up with amazing regularity.

Created in 1955, Piru stores 89,000 acre-feet of water behind Santa Felicia Dam. lake formed is just over 4 miles in length at capacity, and at its widest is about a mile wide. All developments, the marina, launch ramp, parking, and day use areas, have been confined to the west side of the lake. The east side has several coves that have 5-mile-per-hour speed limits. The largest are Santa Felicia Cove and Diablo Cove. Santa Felicia is noted for the large amount of brush in the upper end of its two arms and is a favorite haunt of anglers during spring and summer. The other place where large amounts of brushy cover is found is the upper end of the lake.

Piru is one of the few Southern California lakes with a bass population that is entirely northern-strain, not Florida-strain or hybrid. While northern-strain bass don't grow as large as Florida bass, their willingness to sample a wide variety of lures and flies and their slightly better tolerance of colder water temperatures make Piru a good year-around bass lake where the average angler stands a chance of catching a fair number of nice fish on any given day. The lake record is a very respectable 13 pounds. A 12-pound, 8-ounce bass was taken at Piru in the summer of 1995.

One of the things that should make Piru attractive to fly fishers is that northern-strain largemouth are aggressive, and under the right conditions, a top-water presentation with a floating popper or deer-hair bug can call them up from several feet down. They work best around and over grass beds, rock piles and near brush, especially in low light, making the first hour in the morning and the last hour in the evening prime top-water times.

The best thing about Piru is that it's a fun lake of a manageable size with a little bit of everything to offer the bass angler.

The top-water bite at Piru, however good, usually shuts off pretty quickly in the morning, particularly in the summer, but that's OK because fishing continues to be good right through the day. You just have to switch to a sinking fly. I would recommend starting your morning near the swimming area north of the marina on the west side of the lake. There are some really good creek channels and flats there, just to the north of the swimming area as you go into the narrows. Those flats have deep-water access nearby, and they are good places to fish.

In addition to coves with cover, Piru has plenty of steep, rocky shoreline. This is particularly true near the dam and in the narrow upper part of the lake leading to the north end. These steeper parts with direct access to deep water can yield excellent fishing in the winter and spring. The upper end also has nice brush and old creek channels.

Car-top boats and other small craft, perhaps a float tube, might be an advantage when the lake is full for reaching back into the dense brush at the upper end of the lake where Piru Creek comes in. Float tubes are a recent introduction at Piru. Their use is restricted to Reasoner Cove, where the launch ramp is, and within 100 feet of the shore on the west side up past the swimming area and into the 5-mile-per-hour area on the upper end of the lake, where The Narrows pinches the lake.

Piru's only drawback is that it is not a aqueduct reservoir, but operates strictly on runoff from winter rains and undergoes a fairly deep drawdown each fall to support local agriculture. The lake level normally drops around thirty feet in late fall into early winter, and in the past has dropped drastically some sixty feet. When the water level is down in the winter, fishing can be a bit tough, but when the water is up, there is every kind of cover a bass could want. Low water levels are not likely to occur during El Niño years, which typically experience abundant rainfall. Still, anglers who learned some good spots during the spring and summer should be prepared to find all their best spots high and dry in the late fall and through the winter.

The fall can be a very good time to fish Piru. In the fall, the United Conservation Water District, which controls Lake Piru, is letting a lot of water out, which moves the fish out of the brush in the north end and down toward the deeper part of the lake near the dam. Normally the south wind comes up around 10:00 A.M., creating a lot of mud lines around the lake, and the bass move into the discolored water to feed.

Piru has an adequate launch ramp, as well as a marina with a bait-and-tackle shop. There is also a restaurant snack bar that serves breakfast, lunch, and dinner. Launch fees are $7.00, with a $60.00 annual permit available. Vehicle entry fees for day use also are $5.00, again with a $50.00 annual permit available. Boats must be a minimum of 12 feet long. Some inflatable boats and float tubes allowed, but so-called "personal watercraft" are not permitted. Water skiing is allowed.

The marina has boat rentals. Weekend rental rates are $25.00 per day for a boat with no motor, $50.00 per day for a boat with motor, and prices are reduced by 20 percent from Monday through Thursday. Slips are available, along with dry storage. Fuel is available, both premixed and unleaded.

Catch limits are 5 bass with a 12-inch minimum length, 5 trout, 10 catfish, 25 crappies, and there are no limits on bluegills and redear sunfish. A valid fishing license is required. For information, the marina number is (805) 521-1231.

The camping facilities are very good, with free showers, and campers, trailers, and tents all are welcome. There are 135 spaces for $14.00 per night in the winter, $16.00 in the summer. If you want power, 106 spaces that have electricity rent for $19.00 per night, and 5 spaces with full hookups for $22.00 per night. The campground has water faucets, rest rooms and free hot showers. Reservations are not taken, and it is first-come, first-served. There is a large day use area to go with the swimming beach. For information, contact the main gate office at (805) 521-1500. Services are available in the town of Piru, and there are motels and more services in Fillmore, a few miles to the west on Highway 126, and also at I-5 near Castaic Junction.

SESPE CREEK

SPECIES: Rainbow trout.
BEST TIME: The spring and early summer.
FLIES: Hatches are a mix, but caddisflies primarily. Try Elk Hair Caddis patterns here.
LOCATION: Access to the upper part of Sespe is via Highway 33 north from Ojai to Lion's Camp. The lower end is reached via Tar Creek Trail (a tough hike) north of Fillmore off Highway 126.

According to Jack Spracklin of the Sespe Fly Fishers, a local angling club, Sespe Creek is typical of Southern California streams, which may be among the most productive fishing streams in the state in biomass per mile. The fish may not be large, but "we get 100-fish days on the Sespe, and you can do the same thing in Lockwood Valley," he said.

Sespe Creek is a total of 55 miles long and is a tributary of the Santa Clara River, which is ruined as a fishery and no longer gives access to the sea for steelhead. Sespe Creek remains as the prime and perhaps the only possible steelhead-rearing habitat left on the Santa Clara River drainage. The creek was included in blanket regulations mandated by the National Marine Fishery Service governing steelhead because it has rainbow trout that have a genetic relationship to steelhead. Hatchery stocking was suspended to prevent dilution of this gene pool. What effect that will have on the existing fishery is anybody's guess.

The Sespe is one of those rarest of the rare in water-hungry Southern California, an entirely free-flowing and unspoiled river. Fifty-one of its 55 miles lie within the boundaries of the Los Padres National Forest. Sespe also is designated as a Wild Trout stream. Above its confluence with Alder Creek, the Sespe is open all year, with a 5-fish limit. Below Alder it is a zero-kill fishery from the Sunday preceding Memorial Day to December 31, with only artificial flies or lures with barbless hooks allowed.

Piru Lake is typical of the canyon reservoirs of Southern California. It lies in steep terrain north of Los Angeles. Fluctuating water levels and wind influence angling success.

"The lower section of the Sespe holds the bigger fish," said local guide Randy Weir. "There are lots of big, deep pools, and you can catch fish in there year around" The area is accessed through the town of Fillmore off Highway 126, and Weir notes it's a long hike of about 7 miles up and over the ridge, then down to Sespe Creek on the Tar Creek Trail.

"It's pretty vertical near the end, but the water down there is unbelievable," Weir laughed. "The Beaver Camp area also can be good at times." The main access is off Highway 33 at Lion Campground.

"Most of the fishing here is with dries. Elk Hair Caddis will work just about anywhere. I tie a pattern I call the Sespe Special," Weir said. "It's just an Elk Hair Caddis with a rusty-brown body. It has a dark elk-hair wing, and I add some blond elk hair and a bit of poly to make it stand out. If I can see it easily, it's a much more effective fly. I fish mostly a size 14."

Sespe "hasn't been degraded and channelized, as most of our other creeks have," notes Alasdair Coyne, head of the Keep Sespe Wild Committee, a citizens' group that was formed in the 1980s to keep the designation of part of the Sespe as a Wild and Scenic River. "Keep Sespe Wild has anglers among its members, but also includes hikers, mountain bikers, hunters, rock climbers—all sorts of people use the Sespe. We've been fairly successful...and in recent years have become involved in watershed [improvement] issues such as getting rid of tamarisk on the creek." Anglers and other citizens interested in receiving the free Keep Sespe Wild Newsletter can write to Keep The Sespe Wild Committee, P.O. Box 715, Ojai, CA 93024.

THE LOCKWOOD VALLEY

SPECIES: Rainbow trout.
BEST TIME: Open all year, best in the spring and early summer.
FLIES: Generics. Try an Adams, and also caddis patterns.
LOCATION: Take Highway 33 to Lockwood Valley Road from the Ventura area. From Los Angeles, go north on Interstate 5, then turn west at the Frazier Park exit.

The surprise streams of Ventura County lie in the Lockwood Valley area, nestled in the Los Padres National Forest near the northern boundary of the county. Almost unknown to anglers from other parts of the state, Lockwood Valley has Lockwood Creek, Reyes Creek, and the upper reaches of Piru Creek. General fishing regulations are in effect for all these streams. This is rugged country on the edge of the Chumash Wilderness Area. Its streams are full of small but wild fish, and offer scenic beauty of a type you find only in the coastal mountain ranges.

"The farther back you go, the better it gets," said Randy Weir. "The upper Piru runs year around. So does Lockwood. Reyes Creek is part of the Lockwood Valley area. It isn't real big. They plant near the campground, but you can hike Reyes Creek for miles and find wild fish."

As is the case with the majority of Southern California streams, the farther away from civilization you get, the better the fishing. Some Lockwood Valley streams have easy-to-access sections, but a fair number require a decent hike to reach good fishing. We've arrived at the point in this state, particularly in the southern half, where population density simply overloads the capacity of wilderness areas anywhere close to a paved road. Even if all you encounter are other fly anglers or day hikers, it can be distracting at best on many waters unless you are willing to outwalk the others.

Reyes Creek is one that benefits from an extended hike. The wild fish in Reyes Creek form a unique fishery, according to Maurice Cardenas, a DFG biologist from Ventura. Fish in the upper stretches look like a golden trout. The genetic markers are a bit different from the hatchery fish and the wild fish in other streams nearby. The Reyes Creek trout don't get very large, and Cardenas thinks they may be a rainbow-golden hybrid. He noted the department has some old records that indicate goldens were stocked at Reyes a long time ago.

The other streams in the Lockwood Valley area, Lockwood Creek and the upper reaches of Piru Creek, flow the year around, and while not unknown, offer at least some respite for the fly fisher who wants some peace and quiet while fishing.

You pay for solitude with vigilance. Everybody who has ventured into the area will warn you that anglers contemplating a day hike or overnighter here should be prepared for emergencies. Local search-and-rescue teams spend a lot of time extracting citizens from the Los Padres National Forest.

LAKE CASITAS

SPECIES: Florida-strain largemouth, redear sunfish, hatchery trout in the winter.

BEST TIME: The winter and spring. Trophy bass seekers should try during the cool months, when trout are stocked. The really big bass hunt the trout.

FLIES: Really big streamer flies. Most trophy bass caught by conventional tackle anglers come on nine-inch-long wooden lures. Crayfish patterns fished deep may also work.

FLOAT TUBES: No. Also no wading or other body contact with water.

LOCATION: Take Highway 101 north from Los Angles to Highway 33. Turn Left on Highway 150 and follow the signs to the entrance.

As famous for giant trophy largemouths as Castaic, Lake Casitas near Ojai is a sprawling 3,000-surface-acre reservoir operated by the local water district. It has many arms and coves, plus a large island in the middle, which combine to make some 33 miles of shoreline available to the angler. Casitas was stocked in the 1950s with northern-strain largemouth bass, catfish, and panfish. Trout were planted in the winter. Casitas was a good, but not outstanding bass fishery.

That changed in 1968 when Casitas got the shot in the arm that would turn it into a trophy bass factory. The California Department of Fish and Game put Florida-strain largemouth into Casitas. The lake record was set in 1976 at 15 pounds, 1 ounce, and that was raised to 16 pounds, 14 ounces in 1979. These were not isolated cases either. New lake records were being

written before the ink was dry on the last entry. On March 4, 1980, Ray Easley, a fireman from Fullerton, California, was fishing a live crayfish at Casitas when a huge fish picked up the bait. It battled Easley for several minutes. When it was weighed, it bent the needle at a fantastic 21 pounds, 3 (plus) ounces.

Casitas became the spot to be. You practically could walk across the lake on the bass boats operated by would-be record breakers and the TV and magazine crews covering them. Lots of large bass were caught, but nothing that came close to Ray Easley's monster.

"Casitas got hammered very hard at a time when the theory was to harvest some big fish to allow room for growth of other bass," said Dan Kadota. Well known as a Southern California trophy bass specialist, Kadota is a tackle rep, radio show host, and very serious angler. "Catch-and-release was not prevalent, and most of the really big bass caught wound up on living room walls."

As the number of big bass dropped off, many anglers looked elsewhere. New lakes like nearby Castaic were being stocked with the twin producers of giant bass—Florida-strain largemouth and hatchery trout. Casitas slowly faded in peoples' imagination as the place to catch a potential record breaker, and if that wasn't enough, several years of poor rains dropped the lake level drastically. A few regulars still caught large bass, but they kept their own counsel, and most anglers figured Casitas was a has-been bass lake.

That has changed dramatically. Given enough water, Casitas has the potential to be a prime fishing spot for Southern California fly anglers. It has the standard mix of coldwater and warmwater fish common to Southern California: bluegills, redear sunfish, crappies, bass, and in the winter months, hatchery rainbow trout. Because of its low elevation and mild winter climate, Casitas is an excellent winter lake. If you have a boat and an adventurous mind, winter fly fishing for bass near the 20-pound mark should get your immediate attention.

This lake still produces some of the largest bass in a state known for giant bass, but as Jack Spracklin, president of the Sespe Fly Fishers says, "We call it Lake No Fish." The reason is that, to date, nobody has figured out the combination of tactics and flies that will entice bass who that think a 9-inch trout is an appetizer, not a meal. The man or woman who does is very likely to end up in the record books. Another problem is that shore access is severely limited, and a firm rule prohibiting body contact with the lake prevents float-tube angling, but also keeps water skiers and jet skis off the lake, a fact appreciated by most serious anglers.

Located in rolling hills 78 miles north of Los Angeles and 12 miles from the city of Ventura, Casitas is operated by the Casitas Municipal Water District. Open year around, it has both day use and overnight facilities. Day use is $6.50 per vehicle from 5:30 A.M. to 8:00 P.M. Camping fees are $12.00 and $14.00, depending on campsite location. RV sites are $18.00, and the boat launch fee is $5.00. There are two launch ramps. For Information on use and camping, call the office at (805) 649-

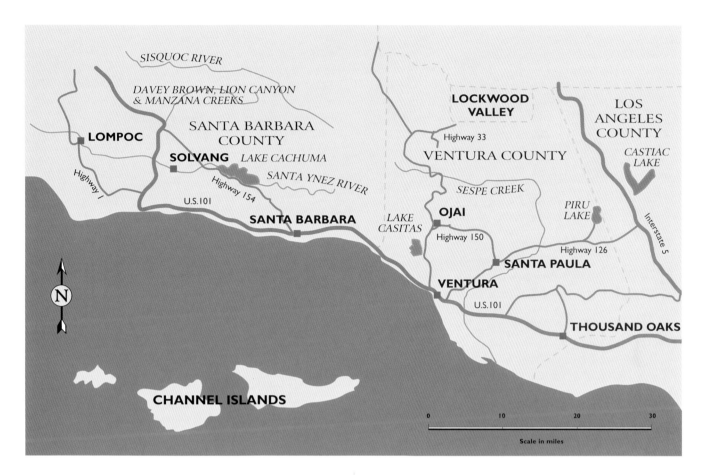

2233. There is a full-service marina operation with 300 boat slips, rental boats, gas and oil, bait and tackle, and a maintenance shop. The marina number is (805) 649-2043.

LAKE CACHUMA

SPECIES: A smorgasbord of northern-strain largemouth, Florida-strain, and hybrid largemouths, plus smallmouth bass, redear sunfish, crappies, bluegills, and hatchery trout.

BEST TIME: All year. Lake is at a low elevation and is good in the winter.

FLIES: Almost anything will work for one species or another.

FLOAT TUBES: No. No body contact with the water is allowed.

LOCATION: Cachuma is about 110 miles north of Los Angeles. Take Highway 101 north to Highway 154, then follow 154 to the lake.

Of the northern-strain bass lakes in the southern half of the state, Cachuma is the largest and perhaps the most beautiful, but because it is located well away from the Los Angeles area, it doesn't get the publicity or the fishing pressure of the other "C" lakes, Casitas and Castaic. Cachuma is a narrow, twisting, 3,000-surface-acre lake set in the oak-covered coastal foothills near the town of Solvang in the Santa Ynez Valley.

Cachuma has had its water problems, which were partly solved by the introduction of California Aqueduct water starting at the end of 1996. But the accidental stocking of the lake with striped bass apparently is not likely to occur as a result, as it has at other lakes, according to naturalist Neal Taylor.

"We have been assured that stripers will not be able to get through the special filtering system." Taylor said. "The system will not allow any living organism to get through the filter, including the zebra mussel, as well as striped bass eggs or fry. It's a sand filter system with no possible bypasses."

The largemouth bass in Cachuma have been increasing steadily in size, and the lake record is 17 pounds, 9 ounces. "That's way too big for just northern-strain fish," Taylor noted. Brush growth around the shore during the drought was of great benefit once the water came back up, providing cover for smaller fish, but it was action taken during the drought to preserve fish populations that really made the difference in improving the fishery.

"We installed about 80,000 square feet of man-made structure," Taylor explained. We used milk crates wired together to form structure elements. We got help from some of the bass clubs, and the Braille institute of Santa Barbara wired the crates together to form the structures. We also used Berkley Fish-Hab, and we tried to get it placed so it provides 'roadways' between the larger milk-crate systems for the small fish. Structure of the natural kind, like a rock or a tree stump, is OK for larger fish, but baby bass and other small fish need places to hide where the larger fish can't get at them. Rather than losing fish during the drought, we actually gained in numbers."

"Cachuma is a classic bass lake," said Dan Warme. A bass pro and the host of a series of "Bazz Clazz" (conventional tackle) videos detailing tactics on Southern California lakes, Warme spends as much time there as his schedule permits. "It's got every kind of structure you can think of—grass beds, trees, lots of deep structure breaks. There's a deep channel that runs the length of the lake. There's big flats. Cachuma offers a little something for everybody. If you wanted to pick a lake you could use to teach yourself bass fishing, it would be Cachuma."

One of the things Warme likes the most is that Cachuma always has been a lake where anglers can throw the fun baits. He thinks it is not necessary to attack Cachuma with fussy little finesse baits. On many other Southern California lakes, finesse presentations have become almost mandatory because of the pressure.

"The fun stuff [for conventional-tackle anglers] is rip baits, top-water lures, crankbaits, and spinnerbaits," Warme said. "Cachuma is a great lake for fishing crankbaits and spinnerbaits. It's also a good jig-'n'-pig lake. Just about anything will work at some time of the year."

For those who don't understand hardware, this analysis of the wide-open flavor of the bass fishing at Cachuma simply means you can readily experiment with all kinds of flies and probably catch something. With simple patterns like the Woolly Worm and Woolly Bugger, you can imitate any number of insects, including damselfly and dragonfly nymphs. Imitations of the adults will work, as well. Northern-strain largemouth and smallmouth bass readily attack surface flies. Poppers, hair bugs, and frogs are all worth considering.

Subsurface patterns like variations of Clouser Minnows and any of Whitlock's shad flies will work well, since shad form a big part of the diet for Cachuma bass. Because crayfish also are a prime forage for both largemouth and smallmouth, make sure your fly box includes some red or orange flies with a hint of olive green, yellow, and brown. I personally like an orange-and-brown Marabou Muddler as a crayfish imitation.

Although fishing is good year-round, September often is a red-hot month for bass at Cachuma. The shad then are small, but a shad-colored streamer will take fish. As you get toward the end of the month, I would recommend a bluegill color, instead. Some anglers report catching twenty to twenty-five fish a day by fishing deep-running streamers a ways off shore, just ticking the bottom.

Like most bass anglers, however, my favorite time of the year for Cachuma (and almost everywhere else) is the spring. Although this is a steep and deep canyon reservoir, in the spring the best fishing is found on the shallow flats that dot the lake. Shallow bass are easier to catch, and you can use a wider variety of flies and techniques to catch them, including floating lines and surface patterns. Local guide Howdy Bernth, who has fished Cachuma for something like thirty years, mentioned to me that the spawn takes place a bit later than some of the other lakes, noting that April, May, and June are very good months for Cachuma.

Bernth said the key to good top-water fishing as late as June is that Cachuma often has cool, foggy mornings, and that creates the ideal environment for good surface fishing. Throwing the standard top-water fare such as cork or form poppers and minnow-shaped pencil poppers in shad colors is very productive over the weed beds as they develop in the late spring and summer.

Neal Taylor, a fly angler himself, notes that while the fly fishing for bass is very good at times, the lake gets little pressure from fly anglers. He also said that they overlook some quite good trout fishing, especially in the fall, when the trout roam the shallows looking for terrestrial insects and scuds and chasing threadfin shad. He suggests anglers pay more attention to these stillwater delights, and I agree with him.

Taylor says one good pattern is a threadfin design he creates out of Fishhair and Flashabou with an epoxy head and with prominent eyes. He ties all these flies in the same light colors, then colors them with waterproof marking pens to "match the hatch" because the shad develop different colors as the grow. This, I might add, is a great way to change the colors and markings on foam and cork poppers, and in fact on almost any fly that will take the ink.

Cachuma is open year around. Fuel, food, bait, and tackle are available. The day use fee is $5.00, the boat launch fee is $5.00 daily, and annual permits are $40.00. Boats must be at least twelve feet long. Catch limits are 5 bass with a 12-inch minimum and 25 crappies. There is no limit on redear sunfish and bluegills. For more information, write or call Lake Cachuma, Star Route, Santa Barbara, CA 93105, (805) 688-4658 For boat rentals, call (805) 688-4040. The number for the Cachuma Store is (805) 688-5246.

THE SANTA YNEZ RIVER

SPECIES: Rainbow trout, some smallmouth bass.
BEST TIME: The late winter and spring.
FLIES: Caddisflies, small general-purpose dries and nymphs.
LOCATION: Near Lake Cachuma, northwest of Santa Barbara. Take Highway 101 to Highway 154 north to Paradise Road. The stream is planted by the DFG from the Los Prietos Ranger Station upstream.

The Santa Ynez River actually is a small stream, mostly containing planted rainbows with some holdover fish. Of interest also are the smallmouth bass, which have entered the system from Lake Cachuma. They don't get very large, but except for the Kern River below Lake Isabella and a portion of the Colorado River south of Parker Dam, there are no other streams in the area covered by this guide where you can fish for smallmouth in running water.

The Santa Ynez also has a number of tributaries that have trout. As you get closer to Cachuma, you probably have a mix of resident fish and hatchery fish, but as you get beyond Gibraltar, a smaller reservoir upstream from Cachuma, the balance begins to shift in favor of resident fish. Even farther upstream, anglers will encounter Jameson Reservoir, which is also fishable for trout. The Montecito Water District allows access to the reservoirs, and the stream. Gibraltar is open for fishing during the winter months, and general regulations apply. For more information call the district at (805) 654-5387.

Best in late winter, spring through early summer, the upper Santa Ynez is primarily fished by local anglers. It gets little outside pressure. High water during the rainy season can block Paradise Road. Call ahead to Los Prietos Ranger Station, (805) 967-3481.

DAVEY BROWN, LION CANYON, AND MANZANA CREEKS

SPECIES: Rainbow trout.
BEST TIME: From the early spring to early summer.
FLIES: Generic types, such as the Adams, Humpy, and so on.
LOCATION: Northeast of Santa Ynez and Solvang. Take Highway 154 to Armour Ranch Road. Turn onto Baseline Avenue, then turn again at Happy Canyon Road north to Davey Brown camp.

Davey Brown, Lion, and Manzana Creeks are a lot of fun. They are very small, and have a lot of brush, and are good for nymph fishing in the larger holes. There's not a lot of room to fly cast on these streams. This trio of small waters all used to get hatchery fish from the state, but in late 1997, I was informed that stocking of these waters might cease because of a ruling by the National Marine Fishery Service. A year later, they were still being stocked, and this was still subject to change. As they are now, the streams provide some good action for local anglers during the spring and early summer months. General regulations apply here, as well.

THE SISQUOC RIVER

SPECIES: Rainbow trout.
BEST TIME: Winter, spring, and early summer.
FLIES: Caddis, Adams, Blue Quill, all very small.
LOCATION: In remote country within the Los Padres National Forest. Hike in or horse pack via trails from Davey Brown Campor over the Sierra Madre from Cuyama Valley.

The Sisquoc lies right in the heart of the Los Padres National Forest. According to Lake Cachuma naturalist Neal Taylor, the Sisquoc is very much a stream for dedicated anglers willing to hike. There are no roads into it.

"It takes a two-day commitment to fish the Sisquoc," said Maurice Cardenas, the DFG biologist. "You will have to spend the night there. It's in wilderness, and you either back pack or take a pack horse in. It's tough."

The Sisquoc has some of the most magnificent wild trout you would ever want to see. According to Cardenas, the stream contains a strain of steelhead unique to Southern California. The fishing is sometimes quite good, but it requires not only hiking, but competent fly fishing skills. These are wild fish and are not easily fooled. Small caddis patterns, Pale Morning Duns, and Blue Quills work, but nothing should be much larger than a size16, according to Neal Taylor. General regulations apply.

Anglers should watch out for poison oak and rattlesnakes. The river runs year around, but midsummer isn't the time to be in there. DFG no longer plants fish in the upper Sisquoc, and the department has been doing studies there. "A lot of people thought the fishery needed to be augmented, but when you look at this pristine water system with no dams or diversions on it, it becomes kind of hard to see the need to plant it," Cardenas said. "Because of the remoteness, the Department's wild-trout crew decided it did not need protection."

There undoubtedly are other freshwater fly fishing opportunities in Ventura and Santa Barbara Counties, but this short list should be enough to get you started. A Los Padres National Forest map and/or good county maps will show all the streams and lakes discussed in this chapter. California State Automobile Association AAA maps are good, and see the Appendix other resources. You can call the Ojai Ranger District Office at (805), 646-4348 to order a Los Padres National Forest map and get current information on conditions. Sources of fishing information include the Sports Chalet in Oxnard, (805) 485-5222, and Bill Calhoon at Eric's Fishing Tackle, (805) 648-5665.

CHAPTER TWO

FISHIN' IN THE CITY

I FELT A LITTLE SILLY. THERE I WAS, CROUCHED under the sweeping branches of an elderly oak tree, sidearming a fly rod at a pond not much bigger than a swimming pool. Behind me, the steady roar of early rush-hour traffic on the freeway enveloped the area. On the other side, two couples stood by their golf carts in the morning mist, watching my seeming fishing-idiot act with considerable amusement.

Finally, the little cork popper landed fairly close to where I intended. I twitched the bug with a two-inch strip of the line and started to think, "Well, that's...." I never got to finish the thought. Instead of the tiny smack of a bluegill inhaling the popper, there was a sound not unlike a bag of cement hitting the pond at terminal velocity. The bug disappeared in a washtub-sized boil, along with most of my nervous system and about four feet of leader.

To my credit, I didn't faint. Perhaps it was the presence of the four goggle-eyed and open-mouthed golfers or the desire to repeat this performance that kept me going. Alas, I didn't get another strike that morning, but two weeks later, another foggy spring morning saw a virtual repeat of the performance. This time however, I was not fishing a light rod and leader, but a 9-weight rod and a bass-bug leader that would have landed a PT boat. The bass wasn't quite that large, but considering it came from a pond my 8-year-old sons could cast across, the six pound fish was still a trophy.

This occurred was more than 20 years ago. The pond, an offshoot of a larger pond in a city park just a block and a half from a major Southern California freeway, is still there, and people still play golf on one side while a few knowing anglers continue to catch an occasional bass and bluegill from the other.

I now live near the wild rainbow and brown trout of Deep Creek and Bear Creek in the San Bernardino Mountains and even closer to a good striped bass lake. For years, however, I commuted daily to my job with a vest, waders, and two fly rods stashed in the trunk of the car. Little ponds and park lakes provided many hours of satisfaction, as well as a number of notable catches in the hours before or after work—not just of bass, but of trout and panfish, as well. This "freeway fishing" is much better than most anglers realize. Many of these small ponds and lakes are managed by counties and cities and a few by private operators. All provide recreational angling for fly-fishing enthusiasts who cannot get away to the Fall River, Yellowstone, or the streams of the eastern Sierra.

In 1985, the U.S. Fish and Wildlife Service conducted a survey and discovered that the majority of Americans who fish—60 percent—lived in urban areas. The figures haven't improved since then. According to the latest studies, more

Largemouth bass successfully spawn in many of Southern California's urban lakes, and provide outstanding (and often very challenging) sport for fly fishers.

than 75 percent of Americans now live in urban areas—either cities or crowded suburbs connected by a web of jam-packed freeways. Today, California is burdened with more than thirty million people, and, frankly, offers poor recreational fishing opportunities for many of them.

However, a lot of new urban angling opportunities that city-stifled fly fishers can make use of have become available in just the last few years, thanks to the California Department of Fish and Game's Urban Fishing Program, part of its effort to bring angling to the urban and inner-city public. The first step was taken in early 1991 in the DFG's Southern California Region 5, when biologists started compiling a list of suitable waters located within urban areas in Los Angeles, Orange, and Riverside Counties that might be used in a pilot urban fishing program. DFG biologists identified over 60 lakes that had potential as sport fisheries in the three counties. Not all of these proved suitable, but the latest version of the Region 5 and Region 6 Urban Lakes Program consists of 27 lakes or ponds. That number breaks down to 15 in Los Angeles County, 9 in Orange County, 2 in Riverside County, and a single body of water in San Bernardino County. Eighteen of the 29 currently are being planted with rainbow trout during the winter months. Similar programs are under way in the Sacramento and San Francisco areas, with a number of lakes and ponds there being evaluated and a few already being stocked with trout when weather and temperature conditions permit.

"This program utilizes more than a million dollars of Sport Fish Restoration Funds annually," said Dennis Lee. Lee is a reservoir research biologist for the state, and recently took over the Urban Fishing Program as well. "The money comes from the Federal Sport Fish Restoration Program and is paid in by anglers as taxes on fishing tackle, equipment, motorboats, small-engine fuel taxes, and other fishing items. The anglers have paid for this program."

According to Lee, about 90 percent of California's anglers live in the four large urban areas: Sacramento-Stockton, the San Francisco Bay area, the Los Angeles basin, and San Diego. The DFG effort so far is aimed at three of the four areas. San Diego, the orphan, already has a Huck Finn Program for urban lakes, plus some of the best bass-fishing impoundments in the world, so the DFG didn't feel they needed to focus as much there as on the other three areas.

"We set aside about four hundred thousand dollars for the stocking program, which should allow planting nearly a half-million trout annually," Lee noted. "We are also utilizing some existing hatchery allotments. We are also stocking catfish in the summer months in some of these spots"

Lee also said the department was looking at the possible use of using Sacramento perch in future stocking programs. "It's our native warm-water species," Lee said. "Sacramento perch are used to alkaline waters and high temperatures, which might

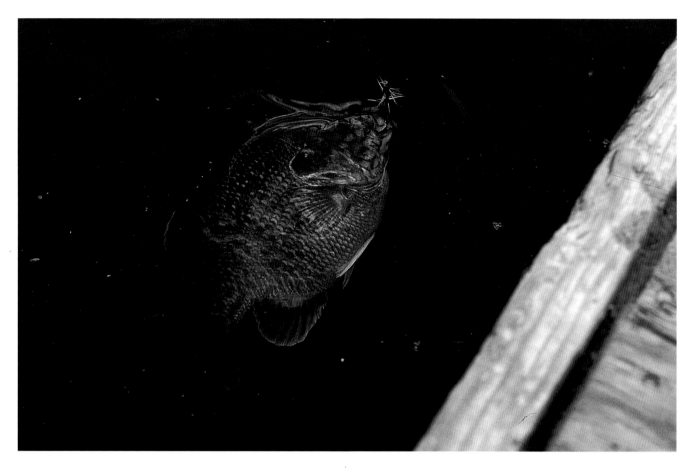

be helpful in providing a fishery in some places. We have specimens being examined by aquaculturists to determine if they would be useful in some of these warm-water programs.

"We also have some small downtown ponds in Southern California that have the potential for outstanding bass fishing. Balboa Park Lake in Van Nuys is one. If you think big bass at Castaic are hard to catch, you ought to try it at some of these urban lakes. There are some quality fish in these ponds."

Despite the fact the trout are hatchery-supplied, these small lakes get so much fishing pressure that the fish not caught quickly become very spooky and are hard to catch. The resident fish, bluegills, crappies, sunfish, and bass, are even harder to fool. They've seen it all—at least in terms of conventional tackle. If there's a bright spot, it's that most haven't seen too many flies, and sometimes a fish that will refuse a live worm will be fooled completely by a Woolly Bugger or a shaggy nymph.

Too many fly fishers look down their noses at such places before they find out how challenging the fishing can be, noting most are operated as put-and-take fishing holes for bait anglers who want to take home a stringer of hatchery trout or a bucket full of bluegills, catfish, or bass.

It is exactly and specifically true that most of these lakes are designed around just such activities, but there's also plenty to interest the angler who chooses to fish with a fly rod, and because they are put-and-take waters, nobody need feel uncomfortable by taking home a trout or two for the table. The bass

Bluegills are common to Southern California's park ponds and lakes. The chunkier individuals are not always easy to catch, but usually a simple fly like a Woolly Bugger will do the trick.

and panfish, on the other hand, are self-reproducing in most of these lakes and should be treated as such by catch-and-release practices. The old idea of cropping the largest bass to permit others to grow into the dominant fish in the pond doesn't work in small waters where anglers are likely to overfish large and small fish alike.

In addition to stocking fish, the Urban Fishing Program is exploring a variety of habitat improvement activities, such as creating artificial brush piles and planting willows.Other ideas that might prove productive are such man-made habitats as Crappie Condos and Catfish Houses, which are constructed from plastic fencing and drainage pipes.

In addition to the small lakes being stocked with trout in the winter, almost every urban area contains county-owned or privately owned and operated lakes that offer challenges to the fly angler who can't get away to more sophisticated fishing. Your local fly shop or sporting-goods store should be able to help you uncover several in your area. Don't be put off by the man-made nature of these fisheries, either. They offer something you can't get elsewhere—fly fishing close by and year around. That alone makes them worth a try. Most of these small waters do not allow boats, and the majority also prohibit float tubes or wading. Those that do allow such watercraft usually are larger county or private lakes that charge a fee to fish. Fly fishing on the hoof is usually not a problem, though. Old clothes and tennis shoes are a natural costume. I recommend a net with a little longer handle than you normally would carry. You often have to reach a bit, unless you want wet feet.

Casting distances usually are moderate, and often you can't get away with a full double haul without snatching the hat off somebody in the background—or worse. The author once hooked a German shepherd on a back cast. This wouldn't have been a major problem, except the dog was in the back of a speeding pickup truck at the time and took him clear into the backing before the leader broke...but that's another story.

Most urban waters that stock state trout during the cooler months are just about right for a 3-weight or 4-weight rod, with the 4-weight getting the edge most of the time. If the lakes also feature largemouth bass, a 6-weight or 7-weight rod and line combo is about all that's usually needed. I like to overload a 7-weight rod with an 8-weight bass-bug taper for tossing big bugs and streamers, but for the most part, a rod from 4-weight to 6-weight is about right for the majority of urban waters. Ninety percent of your fishing can be done with a floating line, but you might carry a sink-tip for larger waters. The same leaders you use for your expeditionary trout angling in the Sierra will suffice in the city.

You won't see much in the way of dry-fly fishing for trout in most urban lakes. Because of the water temperatures in the summer, most urban waters get trout plants only between November and April. Wet flies, nymphs, and streamers are the order of the day for trout. Exact simulation is also not a high priority. Your flies should look alive, and that means using soft-hackles or flies with lots of marabou. In small wets or nymphs, I like the soft-hackles of Sylvester Nemes or scruffy stuff like the Hare's Ear or muskrat nymphs with the dubbing picked out and sprouting in all directions. The Woolly Worm or Woolly Bugger designs are other ideal patterns for urban ponds. Everything from an 8-ounce sunfish to a 2-pound trout and a 10-pound bass will hit them. About the only concession I make to matching the hatch is to use olive flies to emulate the many damselfly nymphs in the ponds.

Forage-fish imitations for urban waters include everything from Lefty's Deceivers on 4/0 hooks for big bass to tiny size 12 Muddlers and Matukas. I particularly favor Marabou Muddlers with lots of white and just a touch of silver flash or tinsel. Two of the biggest fly-rod trout I've ever caught in a urban setting hit Glass Minnows on size 2 hooks that were tied for bonito expeditions to the coastal bays.

The average trout put in these urban ponds by the DFG is around the half-pound or smaller mark, but in many county parks or in privately owned pay-to-play lakes, trout in the 10-pound-plus class often are mixed in with the smaller fish. It's entirely possible that when you hook the biggest trout you'll ever catch, it will be with the noise of high-density traffic and street sounds echoing from tall buildings in the background.

Because of the number of these small ponds and park lakes, I'll not describe individual waters here. The following is a listing of the waters included in the Urban Fishing Program at the time this book was written. Others may be joining the program in future years. For more information, call the Region 5 Aquatic Education Office's information line at (562) 590-5151. Weekly trout and catfish plant information can be found in many Southern California newspapers or by calling the DFG recording at (562) 590-5020.

SOUTHERN CALIFORNIA WATERS IN THE URBAN FISHING PROGRAM: REGION 5—SOUTHERN CALIFORNIA

Some lakes currently are being stocked with trout in winter from November through April. Others are stocked with from January through April. Stockings are twice monthly in season. In the summer, some lakes are stocked with channel catfish. Lakes not otherwise designated usually have resident populations of carp, green sunfish, bluegills, and largemouth bass.

LOS ANGELES COUNTY

CITY	FACILITY
Arcadia	Peck Road Park
Baldwin Hills	Ken Hahn State Recreation Area
Boyle Heights	Lincoln Park Lake
Compton	Earvin "Magic" Johnson Lake
Downey	Downey Park
El Monte	Legg Lakes
Irwindale	Santa Fe Reservoir
Lawndale	Alondra Park Lake
Long Beach	El Dorado Park Lake
Los Angeles	Belvedere Park Lake
Los Angeles	Echo Park Lake
San Dimas	Puddingstone Reservoir

ORANGE COUNTY

CITY	FACILITY
Buena Park	Ralph B. Clark Regional Park
Fountain Valley	Mile Square Regional Park
Fullerton	Craig Regional Park
Huntington Beach	Huntington Lake
Huntington Beach	Green Park Lake
Huntington Beach	Carr Park Lake
Orange	Irvine Regional Park Lake
Placentia	Tri-City Park Lake
Santa Ana	Centennial Park Lake

RIVERSIDE COUNTY

CITY	FACILITY
Riverside	Rancho Jurupa Park Lake
Riverside	Lake Evans

SAN BERNARDINO COUNTY

San Bernardino	Secombe Park Lake

CHAPTER THREE

THE MAJOR STREAMS

DESPITE POPULAR MISCONCEPTIONS, NOT ALL OF Southern California looks like Hollywood. If you drive far enough from the Los Angeles city center, you gradually leave behind freeways, strip malls, fast-food joints, and urban sprawl. Then you discover a singular fact: much of Southern California is empty. A lot of that emptiness is desert and mostly useless to anglers, but there are also stretches of forested, mountainous terrain

Craggy and steep, often with a coating of winter white on their tops, these mountains look down on thirteen million or so Southern Californians. You can stand in the middle of Los Angeles and on a (rare) clear day see with the unaided eye the high-country habitat of bighorn sheep, black bears, mule deer, and trout. Within many of the brush-choked canyons, small streams trickle down through the rocks. There isn't anything in the area that reasonably could be called a "river," even though a number of tiny creeks bear the name. Some of these little streams dry up in the hottest, driest summers, and others barely exist as a few residual pools of water lying in wait for winter rains.

Forests here are not the green and humid jungles of the tropics or the mossy, silent coastal rain forests of the North Coast. Always stressed by the surrounding desert, they may not see rain or snow from March to November. Southern California forests are dusty places populated by plants and animals that are drought-resistant. The upper reaches of Southern California mountains extend well above the tree line, and the densest stretches of timberland consist of old-growth forest with little green understory.

The lower elevations are covered not with trees, but with a thick and thorny accumulation of dwarf oaks, manzanita, and other shrubs that create a hedgelike ground cover of chaparral. One botanical wag called it an "elfin forest," although the Southern California elves must be pretty big and tough, since this stuff can tower 10 feet or more over your head and you need a machete to hack your way through it to reach a stream.

What always startles is the effect that even the smallest streams have on the land. When you do find a creek tumbling down a rocky, brush-filled gully on the lower slopes of one of our mountains, the effect is theatrical, almost like something on a movie set. Maybe there is a little bit of Hollywood in the hills after all. The stark contrast between the narrow riparian area along the water and the arid ground just a few feet away is jarring. These streams seem to run through an alien land.

A surprising number of these special little creeks hold trout. In some, a 6-inch fish would be a tremendous trophy, miraculous just because it exists. In others, planting by the Department

Barbara Bean fishes the lower end of Deep Creek, about two miles from the author's desert home. Even though its autumn, the stream has plenty of water.

of Fish and Game insures you will find a few fish in the 9-to-12-inch range, and if you work at it, you can find yourself cradling a wild brown or rainbow measuring anywhere from 14 to 20 inches in your trembling hands.

In contrast, Deep Creek, near my home in Hesperia, not only runs year around with enough force to be a valuable watershed for several growing desert communities, but has pools in a few places as big as the average three-bedroom home. Usually only 20 to 30 feet in width, Deep Creek is a delightful freestone surprise. A couple of other streams in the region are almost as good, and overall, there's enough stream fishing within a hour or two's drive of the main population centers to keep most anglers happy for most of the year. None of these waters would be mistaken for a blue-ribbon river in the Sierra. Their charm is that they exist, and they can provide escape almost on the spur of the moment, a value not to be taken lightly.

These are all freestone streams, mostly located in steep canyons where they maintain a vigorous descent, dashing down rocky slopes to curve through short, glassy runs or sometimes to widen into a deeper pool. At times, you will find the larger trout in the deep pools and slower runs, but the majority of the trout prefer in the highly oxygenated water of the boulder-filled pockets.

How you fish these small jewels doesn't depend all that much on matching a hatch. Trout in these streams must be opportunistic feeders just to stay alive. Positioning and presentation therefore play the major roles in angling success. During the summer you can wade all of these streams wet, otherwise a pair of hip boots is sufficient when casting in open terrain. However, a good set of chest waders with felt soles often is the best solution if you want to stay dry. Even though I know all too well that most waders are too warm for a July morning on most Southland streams, I usually wind up trying to reach the one spot in the stream that would flood over the tops of hip boots. This isn't because the streams are deep, but because proper presentation often requires kneeling or crouching behind a boulder to avoid spooking the fish or to make an attempt to sidearm a fly under overhanging willow branches.

There's another reason for equipping yourself with the neoprene equivalent of four-wheel drive. You need to get off the beaten track. These streams take a pounding by the public, and not just by anglers. Every stream, no matter how small, gets picnicking families and skinny-dippers, and some of the larger pools on Deep Creek allow people to show off by diving from rocky cliffs. People also appear to have the idea that anything they throw in a stream somehow gets washed out of the environment. I've seen discarded cars, used diapers, beer bottles, stripped lawn-chair frames, even the carcass of somebody's dog in streams here.

The special-regulations sections aren't much better. Too many anglers fish them. Most of the trout in the easily reachable lies have seen enough flies to last a lifetime. So you often

have to work yourself into position in out-of-the-way spots that are seemingly impossible to fish.

Sometimes fishing where others won't is all it takes. Pocket water, for example, so called because the flow splits and reconverges around the rocks, creating numerous tiny pockets of reduced flow that shelter trout, is bypassed by many anglers. One pleasant spring morning a few years ago, with my back wedged against a stout tree branch and the lower half of my anatomy submerged in cool, swirling water, I was contentedly polishing off the last bit of a ham and cheese sandwich. While mopping the last crumbs off my vest, I spotted another angler working his way through the pool below the boulder-strewn rapids where I was lounging.

He was getting a good drift with each presentation, but no trout rose to his fly. After a few more minutes of casting, he left the water, and without glancing in my direction, walked along the other side of the stream to the next pool, reentered the water, and resumed his methodical casting.

I thought for a moment of inviting him to work through the section of rocky, tumbling water I was in, then decided against it. He seemed intent on fishing the pools and bypassing the swifter water cascading down the steeper portions of the small stream. That was fine with me. I slowly worked the yards of broken water between the pools, taking three decent fish and one excellent one.

Pocket water in small Southern California streams with heavy angling pressure often hold fish because in warm weather and

Big Rock Creek, on the desert (northern) side of the San Gabriel range, is one of the little-known streams that add interesting angling opportunities to the Southern California scene.

during the heat of the day, the slower water of pools and flats gain heat from sunlight more rapidly than the tumbling water of steeper sections. Add that to the fact that rocky, quickly descending sections of a stream usually have more oxygen, and it's easy to see that pocket water can produce some of the better habitat for trout in Southern California. Water that looks like it won't hold a single trout is often teeming with them when the conditions are right.

I once took a fat 12-inch brown out of water less than three inches deep on the West Fork of the San Gabriel River. I had positioned myself several yards below a pool where a good fish was rising at the extreme back of the tail of slick water. One of my casts fell a bit short, near a little foot-high waterfall that marked the end of the pool. The fly drifted a couple of feet across the sandy tongue above the fall, and suddenly disappeared. When the brown took, I nearly dropped the rod in surprise. After landing and releasing the fish, I walked up and looked closely at the area. The trout had been lying in a tiny depression only an inch deeper than the surrounding flow, behind a rock no bigger than my fist.

One reason why many anglers choose to fish other parts of the stream is that getting a good presentation and any sort of drift in pocket water is difficult While some pocket water is shallow, larger streams in steep terrain can produce plunging cataracts of white foam that are not only hard to fish, but downright dangerous. The tumult of currents in the disturbed water of even a small stream quickly can drown a fly not designed for it, and the classic, sparsely dressed dry fly is not the imitation of choice. You need to use flies with a lot of flotation.

The opposite holds true for nymph patterns. Trying to get a nymph down in fast water means that weight should be added, and when the target zone, including the total drift area, is only a foot or so long, and perhaps six inches wide, not just any old nymph will do. Good patterns for such short-range, short-drift angling should sink faster than the Chicago Cubs in a pennant race.

Western dry-fly angling has spawned many good patterns for the rough-and-tumble world of pocket water. Most of these over-hackled monsters are unlike dainty Eastern dries in much the same way a grizzly bear is unlike a French poodle. The Humpy is just such a fly. Your first encounter with it in a fly shop is likely to produce an amused grin. What some fly tiers won't try to sell the public!

There it sits, pudgy deer-hair body pulled forward over a wrap of yellow, red, or black thread, with enough hackle wrapped on to float the original rooster that grew it. Usually it's about a size 10 or 12, and about the diameter of a quarter. Go ahead and laugh. It may frazzle a fine tippet, whirligigging in the air on each cast, but it catches fish. You can rocket a Humpy into the tiny strike zone behind a rock or in the funnel of water entering a small pool and it'll cock smartly upright on the conflicting flows. Even if drenched on touchdown, it will pop through the surface film and ride serenely over water that would drown a standard fly instantly.

Another fly that looks perfectly awful, but represents an effective pocket water producer, is the Bivisible. If you like, you can think of it as a Humpy without the body. Dancing along on hundreds of hackle points, it resembles nothing—and everything—to a waiting trout. It won't survive the roughest water, but it's perfect for small-stream pockets and, surprisingly, will do a creditable job in the quietest pools.

Hair-wing patterns float well, too. Sometimes these are designed to resemble mayflies, but the majority of these bulky creations imitate stoneflies or caddisflies. There are dozens of effective and buoyant patterns available, ranging from size 6 Deer Hair and Bucktail Caddises down to the more dainty Goddard Caddis, Elk Hair Caddis, and Trude patterns, which still float well when tied in size 16 or even 18

I'm especially fond of the Trude flies. They use a tuft of rearward-slanting calf tail to produce a wing that both floats the fly and is easy to spot in rough water and low light. My favorites include the Rio Grande King Trude and a offshoot of the Colorado Captain, made into a Trude pattern by lengthening the wing and slanting it rearward. Since calf tail doesn't float as well as the hollow hair from deer and other game species, quality hackle up front is a help, especially in the smaller sizes.

My version of the Rio Grande King uses peacock herl for the body, with golden-pheasant tippet tails and a good brown hackle wound on in front of the calf-tail wing. I used to tie this fly only with white calf tail, but a friend tipped me off to using both yellow and bright orange to produce a fly that could be seen easily in rough water and white foam.

Also useful in fast pocket water are various terrestrial patterns. These become more effective as the season progresses and the stream's output of aquatic insects slows. Imitations of ants, beetles, and grasshoppers all can be designed to float like corks. Just about any hopper pattern will work. Those with generous deer-hair heads and water-resistant body materials work best. I personally prefer Al Troth's Deer Hair Hopper. It substitutes deer hair of one kind or another for everything and is amazingly hard to put completely under the surface.

Beetle and ant dry-fly patterns are so varied and numerous that you pay your money and take your choice. Tiny beetles cut from cork or balsa, sanded to shape, painted, and glued to hooks work well, as do the many deer-hair models. I also usually carry at least a half-dozen miniature Lady Bug flies made from bits of balsa. They are hard to see on the water, but the trout seem to find them easily and like them just fine.

One ant pattern stands out above all others for pocket-water fishing. The McMurray Ant is a perfect pocket picker. Its two sections of balsa body strung together on a short section of monofilament are unsinkable, and it is hardy enough to outlast a dozen fish.

For nymphing in pocket water, I have no specific recommendations about fly patterns. If you like stonefly nymphs or caddis pupa imitations, use them. If you prefer to use only mayfly nymphs, go right ahead. All that's important is that the thing sinks like a rock. That means it must be heavily weighted. I segregate my heavily weighted pocket-water nymphs from the others by adding a tiny dot of yellow paint on the top of the head. This allows me to sort through a box quickly and pick the right weight for a given situation.

But weighting a nymph heavily destroys its natural drifting action. For this reason, the legs or hackle of the nymph must be softer to aid the imitation of life that a good nymph pattern must have to fool trout. Grouse, partridge, and similar soft fibers help achieve this. I use perfectly awful looking feathers from hen backs to get soft, wavy hackle that helps the look of the nymphs I tie. An added plus is that hen backs are as cheap as any fly-tying material can be, and you can get all of the wonderful grays and browns you need for making bug legs that look real.

In pocket water, you also could do well with the soft-hackle patterns written about so well by Sylvester Nemes in *The Soft-Hackled Fly*. These old-fashioned flies have thin bodies of floss, with long delicate legs of soft hackle that twitch and wiggle beautifully in rough water. I use the basic design as the foundation for the majority of my pocket-water nymphs.

Most pocket-water angling with both dry flies and nymphs requires the use of short casts. Most of the time, you'll be fishing not much farther away than the length of your leader. Many anglers prefer a long rod and a light line to keep most or all of the line off the water, just working the first couple of feet of the leader and fly on the water. This is especially helpful when you must spend most of your time crouching or kneeling behind rocks or other structures in the stream to avoid detection.

In very brushy or tree-lined streams, however, a short rod may be better. One of the best pocket-water systems I've used was a dainty six-foot rod with a 5-weight line. The short length let me cast under overhanging limbs, and the whole rig was so light I could fish all day without tiring my wrist. This little combo was a favorite until the day I added a new section to it with a car door. My current rig is a 7-footer for a 4-weight line. I use a short leader, only 6 feet in length, and even when casting from a kneeling position, I can hold enough line off the water that only the first half of leader actually touches down.

If, of course, you are more comfortable with a 9-foot rod for a 3-weight line, by all means, go ahead and fish it on these tree-lined and brush-choked little waters. If anything, not getting all tied up in specialized equipment and a purist mind-set is what fishing Southern California streams should be about. Don Stehsel, founder of the Fisheries Resource Volunteer Corps, a group of private citizens who work with the Forest Service to

Although the majority of the trout in Southern California streams are rainbows, other species can sometimes be caught. Here, a brown trout rises to a caddis on Deep Creek.

patrol, protect, and monitor streams in Southern California, has used bass-class gear on Deep Creek to fish for big, solitary browns that lurk in a few of the larger pools. Throwing a deer-hair mouse on a weight-forward line has produced hook-jawed browns in excess of 20 inches, so you can see there's no such thing as a correct rod, line, or fly for these local waters.

A number of maps are useful for fishing the streams of the Southern California area. First are the various Forest Service maps. At minimum, you should get the Los Angeles National Forest and San Bernardino National Forest maps. You also might want to obtain the Cleveland National Forest map. Check at any Forest Service station or check the Appendix for the district offices. The new versions show all the U.S Geological Survey topographical maps that apply to each area. A good set of county road maps from AAA also will help.

For the better-known streams, there is an elegant set of maps that are as much art pieces as information sources. Called Reel Maps, they are the work of designer Conrad Ricketts and artist Jim Case. Five are for streams in the eastern Sierra, but Deep Creek, San Antonio Creek, Piru Creek, Bear Creek, and the West Fork of the San Gabriel River also are featured. See the Appendix for information on ordering.

Fly fishers venturing into the national forests around Southern California need to be aware of a Adventure Pass fees that the Forest Service now levies. This means that you have to pay $5.00 per day or $30.00 per year to go into the same national forest that was free before. The $30.00 pass is good for twelve months from date of purchase, and for $5.00 you can get a pass for a second vehicle as well. All Forest Service offices and many sporting-goods stores will sell the pass. The pass is undergoing a multiyear test, but I suspect that like so many government ideas, it will be permanent. The idea is to raise additional money for local improvements like trails, camps, picnic areas, and so on, although cynics predict that a large part of any money raised will go to pay the salaries of the new rangers needed to enforce the program, rather than to these capital items.

DEEP CREEK

SPECIES: Rainbow and brown trout.

BEST TIME: Open year-round. The early spring through the late fall is best. Deep Creek often is fishable right though the winter at the lower elevations.

FLIES: Several species of caddisflies are present here, plus a large range of mayflies. Terrestrial insects become important in midsummer. The fish are not particularly choosy.

LOCATION: Near the community of Arrowhead in the San Bernardino Mountains. Deep Creek runs north toward the high desert and the city of Hesperia.

An hour-and-a-half drive from almost anyplace in Southern California takes you through the city of San Bernardino and up the winding staircase of State Highway 18 into the small mountain community of Lake Arrowhead. Branching off on Hook Creek Road sends you down a dirt Forest Service track that reaches the upper sections of Deep Creek. Recognized and managed as a Wild Trout stream by the California Department of Fish and Game from headwaters at Little Green Valley to confluence of Willow Creek, Deep Creek is a delight.

Starting near Arrowhead and Green Valley Lake at the 8,000 foot level, it tumbles "backward" in a northerly direction until it reaches the desert floor near the town of Hesperia. Local anglers know where the various branching roads connect with the stream. The Pacific Crest Trail parallels the stream below Devil's Hole, creating access for those willing to expend a bit of shoe leather to get to the fishing.

Because of its rapid fall to the north as it courses through a steep canyon, Deep Creek is really several streams in one. Beginning as a tiny trickle, it gathers strength from other, smaller streams until halfway down the mountains it becomes large enough to require chest waders if you want to reach the best casting spots at the base of the deepest pools. At the top, it bubbles through huge boulders and passes tall stands of pine, oak, and juniper. Here, it's a typical freestoner, quick and clear, with many tiny trout living in the faster sections. A dry-fly enthusiast can catch dozens of these little fellows in a morning using a handful of patterns. Just about any fly will do.

The fish live in a relatively sterile environment and slash at any fly that appears in front of them.

Not that there aren't good fish in the upper stretches of the stream. My personal best in Deep Creek was a 17-inch brown taken on a caddis just at dusk. The brown lived in a deep pocket formed by two boulders the size of compact cars. It was perhaps 6 feet by 4 feet. Water entered in a sideways rush, glancing off one of the big rocks and swirling around nearly 180 degrees before emptying into the pocket below. The flow had undercut one of the boulders to a depth of about 6 feet. I had positioned myself below the hole on my knees and tried for several casts to get a inch or two of float before the strong undertow sucked the fly down into the dark depths.

On the eighth or ninth cast, using only the leader and a couple of feet of line, the fly bounced off the rock and landed just right. It disappeared in a flash of spray, and I nearly fell into the pool reacting to the strike. Through no skill of mine, the end came when the fish lunged in the wrong direction and slid into the net I had stretched into the water. I cradled the fish in my arms, sliding down into the water until it threatened to slop over my wader top, and hollered at the top of my lungs for somebody, anybody, to come and see my fish.

Distance and the rush of water drowned my voice. My fishing companions all were grouped around the truck, putting away their tackle and discussing the day. I continued to yell until the fish regained its strength, then in the fading light I let it slide through my fingers and disappear once more into the dark water.

I've taken a lot of ribbing from friends over that trout. They know the level of my skill, and most won't admit I'm capable of catching such a fish. In the years since then, it's grown in my memory to nearly 24 inches, and the bright red spots on its side are now the size of dimes.

It's said the majority of the trout you see in Deep Creek are rainbows, but I've always noted a nice mix of browns, as well. You will find lots of smaller fish, with perhaps six or seven inches being a fair average, but there are enough larger fish to make it interesting. If you hike more than a few hundred yards away from the various spots where it is easy to reach the stream, the size of the fish increases rapidly, something that is true for all the small streams in Southern California.

In past years, I've had days where the average fish exceeded 10 inches for a 15-to-25-fish day, and there's always the chance of catching an exceptional fish. As noted, Don Stehsel has taken very large browns with a deer-hair mouse, and I once nearly stepped on a brown that had to weigh all of 6 or 7 pounds. It was holding at the edge of an undercut bank in about a foot of water. It was blind in one eye, and that was the side from which I had slowly slipped up on it. I saw the fish two or three more times in that year, then it disappeared.

You can access the extreme upper section of Deep Creek near the area known as Fisherman's Camp via a trail from Tent Peg Campground in Crab Flats on the east side of the stream. There are other places you might park a car and hike in to the stream, but you'll have to learn these as you go. In the

Fisherman's Camp area, the stream is small, only ten feet or so across in most spots, and sometimes much less.

Probably the most popular section of Deep Creek is accessed from Cedar Glen at Lake Arrowhead via Hook Creek Road to a winding group of Forest Service roads. These dirt tracks sometimes are in very good shape, but have occasional washouts and sections that would challenge a full-blown Baja racer. Hook Creek Road is paved, but soon gives way to Forest Service Route 2N26, a good dirt road. Taking the right fork a couple of miles in will bring you to the T-6 crossing of Deep Creek. At that point you are on Forest Service Route 3N34, which turns into an off-highway-vehicle trail, and trying to cross the stream and head toward Crab Flats to the east is not recommended with anything other than a motorcycle or four-wheel drive.

The left fork heads more or less north to another fork about a mile in. The right side takes you to a parking lot known to old-timers as Splinter's Cabin, an important access point. Until just a few years ago, the cabin was still standing, but it was recently torn down. Here, just downstream, you will find a bridge where the Pacific Crest Trail crosses Deep Creek and heads east into Holcomb Valley. It's from here northward that you can parallel the stream on the PCT for the rest of the length of the creek to where it joins the Mojave River near Hesperia.

Going upstream, you can fish a winding mile or so of decent water with a variety of pools and runs until you reach the T-6 crossing. It makes a nice half-day or evening outing, and you can then walk back down the road, taking a short side road from a point just above Splinter's Cabin and dropping back down to where your car is parked.

If you take the PCT downstream of Splinter's toward Devil's Hole, you will find plenty of good water. The trail climbs well up on the canyon wall, and you have to look for places where anglers over many years have slipped and slid down the steep slope to the water. A modest distance from the bridge, Deep Creek makes a big, sweeping 180-degree bend around a long point. Just beyond that is a good place to drop in and fish your way back.

There are several other such spots. One in particular is where Holcomb Creek enters Deep Creek. In the spring and early summer, the additional flows make Deep Creek below this junction a much better stream. Holcomb Creek itself has trout and, in the spring, is planted by the Department of Fish and Game in several locations in Holcomb Valley.

The next "easy" access is at Devil's Hole. I put "easy" in scare quotes because the last half-mile of this road often is a nasty, rutted nightmare that swallows jacked-up four-wheel-drive pickup trucks. Once, when I had lost my nerve and parked my pickup on one of the switchbacks above, I saw a Porsche parked all the way down under the trees at the end of the road and wondered how he would ever get it out, but that evening it was gone. I've always wondered how the driver managed to get back up that stretch of road.

To reach Devil's Hole, you go left, instead of right, at the fork heading to Splinter's Cabin and go north on 3N34 toward Rouse Meadows. Keep taking the right forks as you go and eventually you will wind up at road's end at Devil's Hole. The last section, from Bacon Flats down into the canyon, is steep, as already noted and at best suited to four-wheel-drive vehicles. However, you usually can negotiate the upper part and park on a turn that has a wide spot. At times, it's easy to reach the water with a vehicle, but each year the road (and the maintenance it gets from the Forest Service) changes.

At the transition zone halfway down the mountain, where the tall trees give way to scrub oak and manzanita, Deep Creek moderates slightly. It becomes slower, and you may find occasional beaver ponds. Here, the fish are a bit more choosy, and finer leaders may be needed to ensure consistent fishing. The fish are a bit larger, too. This section is isolated from road ends and trailheads, requiring a hike on the PCT to reach it.

More years ago than I care to admit, I used to hike with friends from Devil's Hole down to a point near where Coxey Creek enters the Deep Creek drainage. There the trail is not high on the side of the canyon, but only a few meters above the stream and only fifty yards or so away from the water. At that time there were a number of beaver dams creating reed-lined pools that harbored a good number of browns, some in the 12-to-14-inch range. It was a long walk in and out, but the fishing was quite wonderful. I've not been that far in for a number of years, but sources in the DFG tell me that much of the beaver dam area was washed out some years ago. Still, I think it would be worth checking out.

The lower end of Deep Creek exits national forest land and joins the Mojave River drainage just southeast of the town of Hesperia. There's a large Corps of Engineers flood control dam there, and anglers wishing to fish upstream can access the Pacific Crest Trail on the spillway side of this dam, via Deep Creek Road. You cannot park on top of the spillway, as we used to do years ago, but it's a lot closer than having to walk the mile across the top of the dam.

You also can reach Deep Creek from Bowen Ranch, on the east side of the stream in southern Apple Valley. It's best if you have a Forest Service map that shows the dirt roads leading from Highway 18 south to Bowen Ranch. From there, Trail 3W02 leads down to hot springs on the stream that are a Mecca for all sorts of folks. It has a reputation as a party spot for teenagers and what the police still refer to as "hippies," but it also gives you a way to get fairly close to the lower half of the stream. From the hot springs upstream, the fishing is sometimes quite good. It's low enough in elevation to offer better angling in the winter than in the summer.

The lower section of Deep Creek, from the hot springs to the Mojave, holds a few trout, but is definitely not a summer stream. It bakes from June to October, and the water gets warm. The Department of Fish and Game used to stock fish at the extreme lower end many years ago, but that practice has stopped. Still, I would not rule out some fair fishing during the winter, when the upper reaches are snowed in or just too cold for hatches.

BEAR CREEK AND THE UPPER SANTA ANA RIVER

SPECIES: Brown and rainbow trout.

BEST TIME: Late fall through midspring.

FLIES: Both mayflies and caddisflies are found here. Caddisflies are probably more important. Ant patterns and imitations of other terrestrial insects work well in the summer and fall.

LOCATION: In the San Bernardio National Forest, east of Redlands. Access is chiefly via hiking trails.

Not far away in air miles from Deep Creek, but a good drive around part of the San Bernardino Mountains, lies another fine small stream. Bear Creek flows in a curve from its genesis at the dam holding Big Bear Lake to join the upper reaches of the Santa Ana River drainage east of the city of Redlands.

Also accorded Wild Trout status by the California Department of Fish and Game, Bear Creek lives a precarious existence. Much of its water appears to come as leakage around the base of the old dam at its head. Like many small streams, its flows vary widely though the year. In the case of Bear Creek, these can change from less than a single cubic foot per second at its minimum to several hundred cfs at flood stage.

It's a classy little stream, though. Choked with brush in places, it has enough fat brown and rainbow trout (and some say enough rattlesnakes) for several streams its size. It is open all year, and I believe it is much better as a winter and spring stream than at any other time of the year. A few years back, during one of our periods of winter drought, I fished Bear Creek on a warm, shirt-sleeve morning. I caught my fair share of fish, including a number of brown trout in the 11-to-12-inch range. It might have been a typical June morning on any small stream in the eastern Sierra, except this was the first week of January!

Parts of Bear Creek, particularly at the lower end near the remains of Slide Lake, are fairly open, with little streamside cover except willows, but it also has its tough sections, where you need to kneel, crouch, or slink to reach a casting spot, and when you get there, the best method may be to fish downstream, just wiggling out a bit of line with the rod tip. This is true of the upper few miles, accessed by hiking trails from Highway 18, known as the Rim Of The World Highway, between the Snow Valley Ski Area and Big Bear Lake. You also can access the middle portion of Bear Creek from the south on the Siberia Creek Trail, heading for the Siberia Creek Forest Service hiker's group camp.

The area known as Glory Ridge has the most mountainlike riparian area, with Bear Creek tumbling through pine and cedar as well as the willows and low shrubs found in other parts of the stream. The lower sections are much more desertlike.

"I've walked in via the Siberia Creek Trail from the south, where you walk around the mountain to get to the stream," said Kent Heiliger, a member of Deep Creek Fly Fishers. Heiliger has fished local streams in the San Bernardino Mountains for many years. He considers Bear Creek a favorite. "It's a longer way to the Siberia Creek Campground area of Bear Creek, but it's a lot flatter than coming the other direction, down from the highway at Snow Valley. You can see it winding along the side of the canyon as you head down the road [Forest Service Route 1N64] from Clark's Ranch Campground to Bear Creek."

Heiliger noted the trip nevertheless is not without its ticklish spots. "There's a couple of places where the trail has kind of weathered away, and somebody has strung ropes there. You hang onto the ropes and walk across the bad spots. Bear Creek is fairly heavily overgrown in the Siberia Creek area, and it's hard to get a cast in. The trout are small there, and the stream is only about eight or ten feet across, and it's easily waded. The tough part is the brush growth, which makes it hard to fish."

Most of my experience with Bear Creek has been on its lower sections. There you'll find more open conditions as the stream meanders though a wide, boulder-filled flood plain. There are brushy spots, and a few difficult places, but it's more open, and you get some good dry-fly water. It can be windy, but mornings generally are calm, and this is a fine little stream for 5-weight rods and lighter.

The fish, mostly wild brown trout, along with rainbows whose numbers are augmented by some that must run upstream from the Santa Ana River, where hatchery fish are planted, are not sophisticated. The consensus of most of the anglers I know who fish Bear Creek is that a good dry fly for most conditions is either an Adams or a Humpy, and anything from size 12 to size 18 will work most of the time. You can get more choosy about your fly selection, but it's probably a waste of valuable fishing time. In past years, I've had great days fishing ragged-looking brown-and-white Bivisibles when the flies hatching were a dark gray. The trout either are colorblind or just flat don't care.

There isn't a lot of the stream that specifically requires a sunken-fly presentation, but Kent Heiliger notes that for wet flies or nymphs, he often relies on a Woolly Worm or Woolly Bugger, mostly because a downstream presentation often is necessary, with the angler reduced to feeding line out through the guides (without casting) to drift the fly downstream and then twitch it back upstream. It's not your classic presentation, but it does catch fish. I like to carry a few Muskrat and Hare's Ear Nymphs for this stream.

Actual insect species include most of those found in Deep Creek. Bear Creek is a well-balanced stream with healthy populations of mayflies, caddisflies, and midges. DFG biologists have noted that the upper reaches around Glory Ridge also have a fair supply of crayfish and small sculpins, so imitations of these might produce a few larger trout.

Although close to most of the Los Angeles, Orange County, and Inland Empire cities, Bear Creek is remote in the sense that actually getting to the water requires a hike, except for the lower end of the nine miles of stream. That lower area is known as Slide Lake, although there's no lake anymore, just the remains of a huge rock slide that temporarily dammed Bear Creek. To get there, take Highway 38 out of Redlands east into the mountains. Then take the road to Seven Oaks, a small community of weekender cabins and some resident homes in the area known as Barton Flats, and work your way back to the west until you come to Forest Service Routes 1N54 and 1N09. Take 1N54 until you reach the fork near Clark Ranch Campground, then take 1N64. A mile or so past Clark Ranch Campground, the lower end of the Siberia Creek Trail crosses the road. Parking there and walking this trail will take you to the approximate middle of Bear Creek and the 40-site backpacker's camp at Siberia Creek Campground. Drive past this trail and you wind down into the Bear Creek canyon. There, you can park very near the stream, where you will see a sign displaying the special regulations for the stream: a two-trout limit with a minimum length of 8 inches, barbless hooks only. Fish upstream from there.

To access Bear Creek from the north, take Highway 330 from San Bernardino and head east on Highway 18 toward Big Bear Lake. The upper end of the Siberia Creek Trail is near Lake View Point, just east of the Snow Valley Ski Area. This is a steeper trail that winds quickly down to the campground. Closer to the dam at Big Bear Lake is Glory Ridge, accessed via a dirt road that turns south off Highway 18. It's not marked until you get near the end of the dirt road, so finding it takes some looking. It is shown on the maps as Forest Service Route 2N15.

The map of choice for Bear Creek is the San Bernardino National Forest map, available at most ranger stations and from the Forest Supervisor's Office, San Bernardino National Forest, 1824 S. Commercenter Circle, San Bernardino, CA 92408-3430, (909) 383-5588. Hiking anglers also may wish to obtain two USGS topographic maps, the Big Bear Lake quad and the Keller Peak quad, which show Bear Creek well.

Bear Creek flows into the upper part of the Santa Ana River, which is another tiny, brush-choked stream that can give days of fine fishing. It's tough casting in the dense growth of brush overhanging most of the stream's better pools, but the Santa Ana can be wonderful for the angler willing to crawl and crouch and cast with only a leader and a yard or so of line.

The Santa Ana, which almost certainly had a historical steelhead run, is in its upper portions a pretty little stream with several miles of water paralleling the Seven Oaks Road. It is stocked by the DFG with catchable-size rainbows from the spring through the late fall. On weekends, you will find a number of hardware anglers at the spots where the fish are stocked, but on weekdays, it's pretty much deserted.

In addition to the hatchery fish, the Santa Ana has some resident brown trout. In one spot near some weekend cabins, I once caught a pair of 10-inchers from an undercut bank in a pool so small I had to lie on my side fully stretched out and sidearm a 10-foot cast under overhanging willows to reach them. Both fish were as brilliantly marked as peacocks and wonderfully healthy.

Like Deep Creek and Bear Creek, the Santa Ana is noted for the size and health of something else. Rattlesnakes abound. I've stepped over them (and once directly on one) and even came face to face with a snake while climbing around some large rocks to proceed upstream. Fortunately it was a chill morning, and I backed away before the sluggish creature could react to my presence. I say this not to scare any angler away from these streams, only to note that you should be aware of the situation while fishing any of these waters in warm weather. Watch where you walk and even more importantly where you put your hands if you must climb or crawl to reach a casting position.

The Santa Ana drainage includes the South Fork, which runs out of the San Gorgonio Wilderness Area to join the main Santa Ana just north of Highway 38. It also gets stocks of rainbows from the spring into the fall. It's a smaller stream, but worth checking out.

THE SAN GABRIEL RIVER

SPECIES: Rainbow trout and the occasional brown.
BEST TIME: March through June and October through December.
FLIES: Mayflies (Blue-Winged Olives and Tricos), caddisflies, stoneflies, dragonflies and damselflies. Most generic dry-fly and nymph patterns work well. The trout are not terribly selective.
LOCATION: On State Highway 39, north of Azusa. Take Interstate 210 (the Foothill Freeway) to Highway 39 north.

To the west of Deep Creek and Bear Creek in the Los Angeles National Forest area lies a picture-book stream with a long and troubled history. Stretching 7 miles, from Cogswell Reservoir to where it joins the North and East Forks, the West Fork, the West Fork of the San Gabriel River is well known to anglers. Most of Southern California's fly fishers have fished the West Fork, and perhaps a majority learned their initial skills on that short section of water. Its upper reaches, just over 5 miles in length, were the first waters in Southern California to be designated by the Wild Trout Program as no-kill fishing zone.

The San Gabriel once contained a run of wild steelhead, but it has been regarded by water managers not as a stream, but simply as a conduit. The lower river was channelized into concrete drainages for flood control, and dams turned the free-flowing river system into a series of short, disconnected sections.

The West Fork, like the lower sections of Deep Creek, is at a low enough altitude to permit fishing throughout most of the winter months, and the river is open all year. In warm, dry years, the best angling often is in February and March, before the heat of spring sets in. One of the major attractions of the stream is the paved road running from a locked gate at the highway parking lots to Cogswell Dam. On foot, it's 7 miles in and 7 miles out, but although cars are prohibited, bicycles are part of many anglers' tackle. It's still 7 miles each way, but a bike makes the trip a puffing hour-long ride in and a blurry, rattling, 20-minute dash back to the parking lot if you have the "right stuff."

Parking used to be free at the highway, but in recent years, the Forest Service imposed a fee on weekends and holidays. That in turn has been superseded by the Adventure Pass. Anglers will not have to purchase an additional parking slip if they have the pass. If they don't, they can get either the $5.00 single-day pass or the $30.00 twelve-month version at the Rincon Ranger Station not far from the parking area.

I used to fish the West Fork regularly prior to the destruction caused by the Los Angeles Flood Control District in 1981. The stream effectively was destroyed as a fishery by the release of some 50,000 cubic yards of silt from Cogswell Dam, killing both trout and insect life. It had been a perfect stream in many ways. Not only was the fishing better than you had any right to expect, but sections looked like the kind of scene you find on fishing calendars and postcards. To be sure, the lower mile or so of the West Fork was littered with people and their residue, but the farther upstream you hiked, the better it got.

Today, the West Fork has recovered to a large degree, although many consider it less than it should be. A number of improvements have been put in place, the most recent being four fishing platforms for handicapped anglers at various spots on the stream. This (and much more) is the result of hands-on efforts by California Trout, local fly-fishing clubs, and the Department of Fish and Game. The latest improvement results from an agreement between CalTrout and the County of Los Angeles to stop the periodic "sluicing" of the West Fork to remove sediments from Cogswell Reservoir. A revised flow regime will be in effect for several years while all the concerned parties work on a long-term solution.

From the parking lot on Highway 39 upstream, it's a short hike on the blacktop to the first bridge over the stream and the junction of tiny Bear Creek (not the Bear Creek already covered above). This Bear Creek, which trickles out of the San Gabriel Wilderness Area, has a population of resident trout, including a fair share of small browns. Right at the junction of the streams, you'll see a sign declaring that heading up Bear Creek will take you into a wilderness area, but I've been assured you don't need a permit to enter it for fishing.

Weekends have entirely too much family traffic to do any fishing in this lower part, which is open to all forms of angling, with people picnicking, sunbathing, and swimming in the pools. Once you've passed the first bridge and Bear Creek, you leave the majority of the nonfishing public in the dust. By the time you reach the second bridge, about 1.6 miles in, where the Wild Trout section begins, you compete for road space mostly with other anglers, day hikers who don't interrupt, and cyclists. The cyclists can be a minor worry. I've had fast-moving bikes approach me so silently that I was startled mightily when bike and rider swished by my elbow with just inches to spare.

Also, don't be fooled by the locked gate at Highway 39. There can be a fair amount of vehicle traffic on the road. You'll see trucks and cars from the electric company and telephone company, the Forest Service, the California Forestry Department, the Department of Fish and Game, the Los Angeles County Sheriff, and a number of private vehicles. I've been told by a well-placed source that far too many people have keys to the gate who shouldn't, and you should expect to encounter moving vehicles at any time you are on the road. I have seen days when there was zero traffic, but I once had to bail off my bicycle to avoid

being run down by a station wagon full of folks going 50 miles an hour on the narrow road.

That first mile and a half of the West Fork is stocked with hatchery rainbows, and if you fish it on a weekday, you can get at the nice water in the upper quarter mile just below the bridge. From just above the first bridge to the second bridge there also are a few good spots. Many anglers walk or bike past these, headed to the Wild Trout section, but the fish here are a mix of wild and planted trout, and I've caught some dandy rainbows in that stretch.

From the second bridge all the way to the base of the dam at Cogswell Reservoir, the West Fork is restricted to catch-and-release and barbless hooks only. I honestly don't know how to describe the angling. I've had 50-fish days, with the odd fish in the 12-to-13-inch range, although 9 inches is more like the average, and I've fished for hours without catching anything more than a couple of 4-inch fish. Usually the angling is pretty good, except for the middle of the summer and the coldest days of winter. If there's been enough rain for Cogswell Reservoir to fill to capacity, winter often sees the river high, muddy, and very cold. If not, the West Fork is a real treat to fish.

A couple of anglers who must have some mountain-goat genes tell me that hiking past Cogswell Reservoir to fish the West Fork above also is worthwhile. There's a small 7-space campground above Cogswell. It's reached from the west off Forest Service Route 2N24.

Many sections of Los Angeles-area streams are shallow and narrow. The best way to approach fish in such water is to keep a low profile by crouching or kneeling.

You can fish the West Fork without wading. A 4-weight or 5-weight rod is about the right size, except for those afternoons when the wind whips down through the canyon. The West Fork contains diverse populations of aquatic insects, including a number of mayflies, stoneflies, and lots of caddisflies. There are also damselflies and dragonflies in the slower sections and small backwaters. Although I've listed a few fly patterns earlier in this chapter, you will find the majority of the fish more than willing to look at any standard dry fly or nymph. I happen to prefer something generic like an Adams, Bivisible, or an Elk Hair Caddis, but you can fish everything from a Royal Coachman to your slickest size 20 exact imitation of whatever is hatching and you will catch fish.

Nymph fishing here is not an exact science. If you want to consult books or spend some time turning over rocks, feel free to do so. I just tie on a Hare's Ear or Muskrat nymph about size 14 and let it go at that.

The West Fork is a stream you shouldn't miss. Aside from its historical attributes—it once held a run of steelhead, and it is the first Wild Trout stream so designated in the Southland—it is a better than expected fishery almost in the shadow of downtown Los Angeles.

The East and North Forks of the San Gabriel, which join the West Fork near the upper end of San Gabriel Reservoir are not part of the Wild Trout Program. are Both of these are smaller streams, and both receive plants of hatchery fish near the highway. The North Fork travels alongside Highway 39 and takes a beating from the public, but the East Fork heads into steep canyons, where there are no passable roads, and eventually joins with the Fish Fork and several smaller streams.

I fished the East Fork many years ago and found it to be interesting, but never found many trout over eight inches in length. A couple of miles upstream from the East Fork Ranger Station there remain sections of old blacktop road just barely discernible paralleling the stream. Several miles upstream is the famous Bridge to Nowhere to which the old road connected, but past the bridge, the road never was completed because of a flood many years ago. Now the bridge stands by itself.

While the DFG stocks the East Fork for a couple of miles around the Cattle Creek area, where there is good road access, above that point, you begin to see wild fish and possibly some that are of native stock, remnants of the San Gabriel's historic steelhead run. In fact, as this was being prepared, the DFG and local angling interests were electroshocking on the East Fork to see if there are any steelhead that have survived the years of neglect. If they did, there may be some hope for restoring the run. The North Fork also gets plants during the spring, but it often runs too low by midsummer to be fishable.

The East and North Forks have to be considered very secondary to the West Fork, but the East Fork does have its charms. For one thing, because there's no paved road past the ranger station, the area you fish has much less traffic. The farther you hike, the fewer people you'll see, and if you fish it on a weekday, I would seriously doubt you'll have much company.

I have never fished the Fish Fork or the extreme upper reaches of the East Fork. In the past, I used to get glowing reports from a guy I worked with about the Fish Fork. He would backpack into the area a couple of times a year and spin fish for the wild brown trout in the steep canyons. He said there were some awesome fish to be found, but that's the extent of my knowledge. I've never found a fly angler who has made the trip.

Bill Reeves, a member of Deep Creek Fly Fishers, told me that his favorite part of the East Fork was at the Iron Fork, several miles upstream from the road's end. He related that he used to get off work at midnight, drive to the end of the road, hike upstream until about 4:00 A.M. to reach the Iron Fork, then fish for a limit of fish (15 in those days) and be back to his car by midmorning.

Anglers thinking of fishing the East Fork in future years should know that the huge fire of the summer of 1997 burned through the upper reaches. The fire started several miles upstream. What will happen to the trout population in coming winter rains and floods is anybody's guess. You might want to check with the Mount Baldy Ranger District at (626) 335-1251 or the Department of Fish and Game's Region 5 office. (See the Informtion sources on page 100).)

SAN ANTONIO CREEK

SPECIES: Rainbow trout, brown trout.
BEST TIME: Year-round, best in the spring and fall.
FLIES: Mayflies and caddisflies. Try Blue-Winged Olive, Adams, Humpy, and other generic patterns. Nymphs like the Peacock, Muskrat, and Hare's Ear Nymph will work.
LOCATION: North of Pomona. Take Interstate 10 to Euclid Avenue, then go north through San Antonio Heights to Mount Baldy Road.

San Antonio Creek to me is what a freestone stream should be—except for the power plants and other man-made intrusions. Its headwaters start on the south side of Mount Baldy and plunge swiftly through the canyon, loosing altitude quickly. The upper reaches are near 7,000 feet, and the lower section is just above 2,000 feet. This makes some portion of San Antonio Creek fishable at any time of the year.

This is a narrow stream, often choked with willows and overhung with trees. You can find some dandy rattlesnakes here, especially in the low-altitude stretches, and both stinging nettle and poison oak can zap unwary anglers. It's also an urbanized stream in one sense: Above are ski resorts and small communities, below are the millions of people who live in the Los Angeles basin. Like the West Fork of the San Gabriel, San Antonio Creek gets a lot of pressure from anglers and other recreation-minded folk.

That said, the fishing can be quite good, although as on most of these streams, a 10-inch fish is something to be ogled and a 12-incher is a true trophy. At the time of this writing, the San Antonio was under consideration for inclusion in the Department of Fish and Game's Wild Trout Program.

San Antonio has both rainbow and brown trout, but the rainbows make up the bulk of the fish, outnumbering browns about two to one. In the latest survey data I have, the majority of the browns are found in the area around Powerhouse #2.

The water generally is clear, and while flow rates vary from as low as 50 cubic feet per second to above 500, there usually is some decent angling all year. This is hiking country, and the trails along the stream often are steep, so wear sturdy hiking boots and fish a light rod: 3-weights and 4-weights are about right. I fish San Antonio and most of the other streams in the area with a 5-weight, but that's only because I have an old favorite I don't want to leave in the closet.

San Antonio offers the essence of quick freestone fishing. The flow rates are high most of the time. The steep gradient assures that the fish get only a minimal look at the food that rushes by in most places. A well-presented fly is going to get smacked if there's a trout there to see it. I won't be so daring as to suggest that the choice of pattern doesn't matter, but as I've been suggesting throughout this guide, pattern matters less than getting the fly in the right spot without spooking the fish in these small streams. Icehouse Canyon Creek, which enters San Antonio Creek above Mount Baldy Village, has a resident population of brown trout. Reel Maps (see the Appendix) has a San Antonio Creek map, and this is a good guide to the fishing there.

PIRU CREEK

SPECIES: Rainbow trout.

BEST TIME: Open all year, but best in the winter, spring, and fall.

FLIES: Several species of mayflies and caddisflies are present. Piru also is a good stream for fishing beetle and grasshopper patterns. An Elk Hair Caddis or Humpy and various terrestrial patterns are all good at times.

LOCATION: North of Los Angeles between Pyramid and Piru Lakes. Take Interstate 5 north to the Templin Highway turnoff, then go five miles on the Templin Highway to Frenchman's Flat Campgrounds. There's a locked gate there, but you have room to park and walk or bike to the stream.

Piru Creek is one of Southern California's better trout streams. It is a tailrace fishery, issuing from the dam at Pyramid Lake and tumbling southward 14 miles to Piru Lake. In 1990, a portion of Piru Creek from the falls about a mile and a half above the locked gate at Frenchman's Flat Campground up to the "big" bridge was designated by the DFG as a Wild Trout stream. In the section below that, also about a mile and a half long, the state still stocks trout, and the stream is under general regulations, so you can catch and keep a fish for the pan if you desire. The falls, created by a broken-down concrete culvert, act as a natural barrier to the upstream movement of the hatchery fish and help preserve the special-regulations section as a Wild Trout fishery. Piru Creek is a shorter version of the West Fork of the San Gabriel in that there is a paved road behind the gate for easy walking or biking.

Because it is a year-round fishery, Piru Creek gets a lot of angling pressure. Despite the heavy pressure concentrated on a short stretch of water in the special-regulations section, fishing tends to be very good. Population studies in the late 1980s showed there were plenty of trout, and a more recent survey by the DFG found 6,600 rainbow trout per mile. In an old newspaper clipping, John Deinstadt, the now-retired head of the DFG's Wild Trout Program, was quoted as saying that Piru "will not be a Hot Creek in terms of the size of the trout or the splendid setting, but it should equal Hot Creek in terms of total trout landed per mile of stream."

As Deinstadt said, the stream itself is not a picture-book sort of place. It is not wide, and can flow from a low of around 5 cubic feet per second in midwinter to over a 1,000 cfs during heavy runoff from winter rains. In the summer, the flow is held to a minimum of 10 cfs by agreement with the Department of Water Resources, but generally flows are greater than that. There are lots of trees and tules to reach out and snare your fly, but there also are nice-sized pools and open runs to fish. This is not a stream to fish without waders, for the most part, because the streamside brush limits casting angles.

Piru Creek is a better as a spring and winter stream. The rather low elevation makes this a tough place in midsummer, although it remains open and fishable all year. Almost unknown by the majority of anglers, the upper reaches of this stream above Pyramid Lake also are a year-around stream. See Chapter 1 for details on the upper section of Piru Creek.

THE SAN JACINTO MOUNTAIN STREAMS

Mount San Jacinto is part of the transverse mountain ranges that cut across Southern California. The San Gabriels and San Bernardinos make a sweeping northern barrier nearly from the sea to San Gorgonio Pass, east of Banning in San Bernardino County. San Jacinto erupts from the basin floor, and its tallest peaks reach more than 10,000 feet in elevation. The San Jacinto and Santa Rosa ranges are like a dot at the end of the exclamation point of the San Bernardinos, and fall within the San Bernardino National Forest. Several small communities, Idyllwild being the largest, are situated in these mountains, as are several small trout streams of interest.

The San Jacinto River is the best known of these waters. The North Fork of the San Jacinto is stocked with catchable trout from the spring through the summer. Access is fair, although you might expect fire closures during the summer. (Some anglers who don't mind hiking favor these because they keep people away from the streams.) In general, however, the North Fork is accessible most of the year. The stocking is on a portion of the river that runs near Dark Canyon Campground, just west of the San Jacinto State Park boundary. Take Highway 243 north from Idyllwild.

Farther southwest along the reach of the North Fork, you can find both wild rainbow and brown trout. The North Fork flows for several miles southwest, and there is fair access here on dirt fire roads and off-highway-vehicle trails. Forest Service Route 5S09 takes you to the confluence of Stone Creek and the North Fork. Both offer fair fishing.

On the south side of Highway 74, which runs from Hemet up to Mountain Center, the South Fork spills out of Hemet Lake and roughly parallels the road for a number of miles. This portion of the stream has some large pools and fair riffles. One DFG employee told me he had seen good numbers of brown trout below the junction of Strawberry Creek and the South Fork, and I have caught some decent fish near there in the spring.

The South Fork is accessible from three places. The access point at the lowest altitude is at a locked gate belonging to the local water district. It's on the right side of Highway 74 going up. Please don't park in front of the gate. (As the sign on it says, they'll tow your car if you do.) The hike down to the stream is only a mile or so. You'll be able to see a large water pipe crossing the canyon on a suspension trestle at the junction of Strawberry Creek, Dry Creek, and The South Fork of the San Jacinto.

The next access point is about halfway up the mountain. Forest Service Trail 2E17 leaves Highway 74 at a large parking area. (Don't forget your Forest Service Adventure Pass, or the rangers will add to your adventure with a parking ticket.) This trail winds three miles down to the river and connects with Forest Service Road 5S15. Most people think of this as an overnight hike, either up to the dam at Lake Hemet to catch the trail out there, or downstream to the water district gate.

The third entry point is at Hemet Lake, on the upper end of

the stream. There's also a area of public access on the north shore of the lake. It has parking, a graded road heads toward the dam, and you can hike down to the stream from there.

Tiny Strawberry Creek runs through the south end of the town of Idyllwild. It gets stocked in the vicinity of Highway 243. Some of the fishable sections are among houses and cabins, but the stream soon begins a steep descent. You can fish these areas by driving the four-wheel-drive roads heading to Toll Road Canyon and locating the bridge crossing the stream. Then fish downstream. You also can fish Strawberry Creek where it runs into the South Fork of the San Jacinto.

Fuller-Mill Creek is a trickle, a tributary of the San Jacinto River. It gets stocked in the spring near the Fuller-Mill Campground on Highway 243, a few miles north of Idyllwild. Dark Canyon Creek is in the same area and also is a tributary of the San Jacinto. Both are very small, brushy, and get some attention from bait anglers, but might be worth checking out for the experience.

There is no fly shop in Idyllwild to my knowledge, and local information on these streams is hard to come by. General information and road notes are available from the San Jacinto Ranger District office in Idyllwild, (909) 659-2117. The reverse side of the San Bernardino National Forest map shows this area in good detail.

SOME SMALLER STREAMS

In addition to the prominent streams given individual attention above and the cluster of small streams on Mount San Jacinto, Southern California has a number of lesser waters that the adventurous fly fisher can explore. Most are really small, some have wild or native trout, and a few get stocks of hatchery fish. In wet years, some of these are reasonable sport fisheries, but in the endemic drought that afflicts most of the Southland, a number are on the critical list nearly year-round. I will quickly cover these, giving only the bare minimum of information, leaving you to ferret out these minor fishing spots and see for yourself what subtle beauty and sometimes good angling they contain.

Not far to the east of San Antonio Creek on the south or "front" face of the San Gabriel Mountains you'll find Lytle Creek and Cucamonga Creek. Lytle Creek is a popular recreation destination, and the Middle and North Forks of this very small stream get hatchery fish in the spring through the fall each year. There are wild fish in both forks, but these are upstream a ways. To reach Lytle Creek, take Interstate 15 to Sierra Avenue north of Fontana, then turn north on Lytle Creek Road

Cucamonga Creek is even smaller, and suffers more than most in dry years. A survey in 1995 found both wild and hatchery trout in the little trickle. I've not fished (or even seen) this tiny water for more than two decades, so you are on your own there. Cucamonga Creek sometimes is stocked with hatchery trout in the spring and early summer. Access this stream via Forest Service Route 1N35 out of San Antonio Heights. There are some studies being done on this stream by the wild-trout biologists, but there is no change in regulations in the offing at this time.

The north side of the Angeles National Forest and the San Gabriel Mountain Range looks out over the Antelope Valley and the western end of the Mojave Desert. The northern slopes are dryer than the southern, but even here, you find trout. Big Rock Creek, just west of Wrightwood, is an intriguing little stream. It gets stocked fish in the spring and early summer, but I've caught brilliantly marked 4-to-6-inch fish there that were as wild as nature itself. One fall afternoon, I finished out a cast and, feeling that I was being watched, glanced around to discover a young bobcat, all gawky adolescence and long legs, staring at me. To reach Big Rock Creek, take Highway 138 to Palmdale, then go south on N6 to Valyermo. The stream is stocked from the national forest boundary upstream a couple of miles.

Farther west lies Littlerock Reservoir, also just off Highway 138. It's planted with trout, but I would check out Littlerock Creek above the reservoir, which also is planted by the DFG in wet years for about 5 miles upstream of the reservoir. In drought years, it becomes a series of disconnected, shallow pools and slow runs rising out of the sand and sinking back again. Even in good times it is a minor stream, but a decade ago I sat on a rock and watched a handsome trout of perhaps 12 inches confidently sipping flies off the surface of the creek.

Bouquet Canyon Creek runs southwest from Bouquet Reservoir about 10 miles to the Texas Canyon Forest Service station. It parallels a blacktop road. Listed as a state-stocked water, it is a fair stream for the spring and early summer months. Take Interstate 5 to the Highway 126 off-ramp, then go east to Saugus and turn north. The DFG plants this stream with rainbows in late spring for about 9 miles, and it provides some fair fishing both for conventional-tackle and fly anglers. This is a popular area for recreation, having no fewer than six U.S. Forest Service campgrounds along its length.

Not every small stream within the area covered by this guide is mentioned in this chapter. Some streams in Santa Barbara and Ventura Counties are detailed in Chapter 1, and a very few tiny streams in Orange and San Diego counties are discussed in Chapter 8. Even that coverage does not include every trickle of water that has trout. I will leave a number of very small streams you to discover for yourselves. After all, that's half the fun.

CHAPTER FOUR

THE MOUNTAIN LAKES

TO NOBODY'S GREAT SURPRISE, SOUTHERN CALIfornia doesn't have many high-altitude lakes. It's not that we don't have mountains. Several soar well over 10,000 feet. But lakes here are man-made, and with few exceptions, water developers have chosen the easy way and built reservoirs in the low foothills, where they get maximum drainage from the surrounding watersheds. This chapter details the fly-fishing opportunities on those lakes at reasonable altitudes that provide trout fishing during the warmer months, plus some excellent warmwater angling, as well.

With the single exception of Big Bear Lake, these impoundments are small and are controlled either by county park departments or contract operators. Fees for fishing these waters are not high, for the most part, and while the quality of the angling experience varies widely, the singular fact is that like all Southern California lakes, their very existence is something to appreciate.

Because the winter climate at lower altitudes provides an extensive winter trout fishery for put-and-take angling that lasts through the summer months, we have year-round, nonstop trout fishing. It may not be the equal of the more famous destinations, but it offers reasonably good angling, and these mountain lakes are in beautiful settings.

That's the good news. The problem is the same one that plagues all Southern California waters. There are too many people wanting to use too few aquatic resources. Even if it were only other anglers, sometimes the water would be too crowded, and with all the other recreational uses that Southern California residents can find for its lakes and streams, anglers often are tempted to throw up their hands and start planning occasional trips to Yellowstone or the Sierra. That's not necessary. These waters can provide enjoyable angling and plenty of relaxation as well. You just have to think about fishing prior to Memorial Day, after Labor Day (even that is beginning to change with the advent of year-round school), and on weekdays, when the pressure is lighter.

BIG BEAR LAKE

SPECIES: Rainbow trout, largemouth bass, smallmouth bass, bluegills, crappies, and carp.

BEST TIME: From late March through October.

FLIES: Small streamers, bass bugs, damselflies (adults and nymphs), Woolly Buggers, and most generic dry-fly patterns.

FLOAT TUBES: Yes, and wading also is permitted. Float tubers must purchase a daily or annual use pass.

LOCATION: Big Bear is about 90 miles east of Los Angeles and is reached via Highway 330 and Highway 18 from San Bernardino. Another route is Highway 38 through Redlands and over Onyx Summit. A

Television fishing host Gordon McHenry tapes a brown trout from Lake Arrowhead prior to releasing the fish.

third way into the valley is best for high-desert residents. Take Highway 18 from the Apple Valley-Victorville area through Lucerne Valley and up Cushenbury Grade to Big Bear. Fly-in fishing is made easy by a full-service airport just east of the lake.

It's hard to tell if Big Bear Lake qualifies as an urban lake in a mountain setting or an alpine lake in the center of a overdeveloped mountain metropolis. It's a bit of both, and is one of the most popular recreation spots in the San Bernardino Mountains. Nestled among tall pines at 6,750 feet in the San Bernardino National Forest, this 3,000-acre lake is over 7 miles long. It provides good fishing for rainbow trout, bluegills, largemouth and smallmouth bass, catfish, and crappies.

There is some natural reproduction of trout in a few tiny tributary streams, but knowledgeable estimates are that wild trout in Big Bear Lake amount to probably no more than a few percent of the total number of fish. The streams are closed to fishing during March, April, and most of May to protect what spawning there is, and any fly fishing you might do after that in these tiny trickles would be incidental to the real fishing in the lake itself.

However, the fact that most of the trout are planters should not discourage anglers. The planting of trout on a regular basis by the Department of Fish and Game is augmented in May by the local fishing association for the Big Bear Trout Classic, a charity event. Huge trout up to 16 pounds are planted, and while the event is for conventional-tackle anglers, the fly fisher can benefit by fishing the lake in the weeks just after the event.

Since 1994 , the DFG has changed its trout-stocking program at Big Bear from put-and-take to what it calls "put-and-grow." Thousands of small 2-to-3-inch trout are stocked in addition to larger, catchable fish, often in the fall just before ice starts to form around the shoreline. These smaller fish react to the excellent forage in the lake by growing quickly. Holdover fish a couple of years old often are 12 to 15 inches in length and fleshed with firm, pink meat. They are wild trout in all the important ways and can provide some interesting angling.

Mike Giusti, a DFG biologist who has studied Big Bear, thinks it is vastly underrated as a trout fishery and believes that with a bit of fine tuning it could be as impressive a spring fishery as Lake Crowley in the eastern Sierra. That's saying quite a lot, but in general I agree. Big Bear has much more potential for the fly angler than a lot of other waters that have much better reputations. Big Bear Lake trout are considered by many anglers to be quite a challenge. Conventional-tackle anglers take most of the really big fish by deep trolling, but the persistent fly fisher who understands the conditions can do pretty well.

Because of the elevation, Big Bear warms more slowly than surrounding lowland waters. Trout fishing here is just getting started as the trout fishing "down the hill" in the Los Angeles basin is winding down. April is a good month to begin, and even

the midsummer months of July and August can offer good trout action early in the morning and again in the evening. Anglers need to remember that although Big Bear Lake is at 6,700 feet, it is surrounded by California desert, and the midsummer sun is vicious. Daytime temperatures can reach triple digits on rare occasions, and serious sun screen, long-sleeved shirts, and a wide-brimmed hat are a good idea.

A favorite spot of mine for many years has been the flooded brushy flats in Grout Bay, near the tiny town of Fawnskin. I first fished this area in the late 1950s, when most of it was grassy cow pasture. In those days, the lake normally was only about two-thirds the size it is today. The water was controlled by orange growers in the Redlands-Yucaipa area, and it was drained off nearly as fast as it ran into the lake.

Only in really wet years did the water back up into the flats of Grout Bay, but when it did, the whole area became spawning grounds for huge schools of bluegills, carp, catfish, and largemouth bass. You could wade wet in the furnace heat of late afternoon and catch mega bluegills and bass to your heart's content. If you wore shorts, the bluegills guarding their nests would attack your legs, nipping flesh and pulling hair. It was a bit startling at first, but you soon got used to it. In recent years, the bluegills have been slightly reduced in numbers, but illegally introduced crappies have proliferated, and it's not uncommon to catch a big bunch of these panfish, which probably, to be ecologically correct, should be kept and eaten.

During spring, the shallows along the north shore of Big Bear Lake can reward wading anglers with a mixed bag of trout, bass and panfish.

Remember, however, not to overdo this. The state limit for crappies is 25 per day.

The bass in Big Bear Lake are an interesting case. The largemouths have been there as long as I can remember. The cold winters make for slow growth, but it's not uncommon to tie into a 4 or 5 pound fish a couple of times each year, and streamers or popping bugs fished over the weed beds in the summer can account for a half-dozen energetic 2-pounders in an evening.

The flat, weedy bays at the east end of the lake are particular favorites of largemouth-bass enthusiasts in the summer and fall as the weed beds grow to the surface. Wading or float tubing these at dusk with a fly rod and bass bug is sure to provide some excitement. The current record for largemouth bass is a respectable 7 pounds, 9 ounces, and you might find yourself hooked to a fighting smallmouth over 3 pounds if you play your cards right.

Speaking of smallmouth, they require a slightly different approach. This species of bass is more prone to rocky structure than to weed beds. Boulder Bay and Metcalf Bay on the south side of the lake are potential hot spots. Try any fly that resembles a crayfish, either in shape or color. Orange with a touch of brown or green is a good choice.

The Big Bear Valley Sportsmen's Club was responsible for stocking the smallmouths some years ago. With the Department of Fish and Game and anglers from nearby Lake Arrowhead, they worked out a swap, trading salmon stocks for the bass. There's a 12-inch minimum size limit on bass here, and visiting anglers are encouraged to release all smallmouths caught.

Another fish for which Big Bear has a reputation (and probably wishes it didn't) is carp. The lake is loaded with them. In addition to carp weighing over 20 pounds, there are large schools of brightly colored goldfish up to 3 pounds, probably released by illegal bait fishermen sometime in the past. While some anglers fish for the carp, the majority of the sport they provide goes to the bow hunters. Starting about the end of April, you'll see archers armed with fishing arrows connected to reels mounted on their bows wading slowly through the shallow coves or ghosting slowly along in specialized carp-shooting boats with electric motors.

Most fly fishers turn up their nose at carp, but that's only because they've never caught one on light tackle. The trick is to fish a slender olive damselfly nymph—size 12 is about right—with a cast well ahead of cruising schools of carp.

This is not as easy as it sounds, since carp in shallow water are easily spooked. Let the nymph sink to the bottom, and when the carp get within a couple of feet of the fly, start it up smoothly, like a nymph headed for the surface to hatch. When a carp takes a nymph, it darts forward, and you'll see a white flash at the mouth. Set the hook and hang on!

The semi-urban nature of the lake gives good access to most of it, with a paved highway circling completely around the shoreline. Some areas where houses go right to the water on the south shore are difficult to reach on foot, but most of the lake is accessible. The north shore is more lightly developed, so far, and anglers can find areas where wading along the shoreline will allow good casting.

Fishing from a boat also is an option, but fishing from a float tube is probably the ideal technique—and it's cheaper, since the yearly lake use permit for a tube or raft is less than half of the tab for a registered vessel. I seriously would recommend that anglers wear a high-visibility hat or vest while float tubing. Big Bear is crawling with jet skis and fast ski boats, and you do have to watch out for fast traffic.

The lake has two public boat ramps, in addition to a number of private marinas and launch facilities. Both ramps are open most of the year, except for Tuesdays at the eastern ramp. The western ramp office is open 7 days a week from mid-May to late October.

The lake is operated by the Big Bear Municipal Water District, which charges fees for boat use at the lake. The daily fee for any type of boat is $10.00. The yearly fee for any motorized boat and for sailboats over 8 feet is $60.00. Boats without motors, sailboats under eight feet, sailboards, and float tubes are charged $25.00 per year. The permit year runs from April to April. Seniors over the age of 62 get a discount of $10.00 for motorized craft and $5.00 for craft without motors. Lake permits are available at the public launch ramps, the water district office, and several of the marinas.

The quickest way to get general information on lodging, restaurants, and other essential information is to call the Big Bear Chamber of Commerce at (909) 866-7000. This is a computer voice-mail setup that guides you through a touch-tone menu. If you want to speak to an actual human, try (909) 866-4608. You also can receive brochures on the area by writing to Big Bear Chamber of Commerce, P.O. Box 2860, Big Bear Lake, CA 92315. The office number of the Big Bear Municipal Water District is (909) 866-5796. The eastern public launch ramp is (909) 866-2917 and the western ramp office is (909) 866-5200.

Two sources of fishing information in the Big Bear area are Lin Crawford at Lin's Tackle Box, (909) 866-6260, and Cliff Fowler at Big Bear Sporting Goods, (909) 866-3222. You can find some flies and tackle at these shops, but there is no dedicated fly shop in the valley. However, some distance away, an excellent source of fly-fishing-specific information is Riverside Ski and Sport at 6744 Brockton Avenue, Riverside. The owner, Bob Slamal, has been fishing Big Bear for many years and can offer good advice. The number is (909) 784-0205.

Big Bear Lake has 9 privately operated marinas: Big Bear Marina, (909)866-3218; Boulder Bay Marina, (909) 866-7557; Cluster Pines, (909) 866-2246; Grey's Landing, (909) 866-2443; Holloway's Marina ,(909) 866-5706; Juniper Marina, (909) 866-2940; Pine Knot Landing, (909) 866-2628; Lighthouse Camp, (909) 866-9464; North Shore Marina, (909) 878-4386; and Pleasure Point, (909) 866-2455.

All these facilities are open from the spring through the fall, and the boating angler can find ready access to launch ramps, rental boats, rental slips, fuel, bait and tackle, and just about anything else. Big Bear Lake is framed by three small towns, Fawnskin on the north shore, Big Bear Lake on the south, and Big Bear City to the east. At the east end of the lake, the Stanfield Cutoff, a road atop a dike, connects Highway 18 on the north shore to Highway 38 on the South Shore. As you go west on Highway 18, you'll past a number of public and Forest Service facilities, including boat ramps, camps, and stores. The town of Fawnskin has restaurants, lodging, and gas, plus stores and post office. The south shore, including Big Bear Lake and Big Bear City, is much more urbanized, with shopping centers, motels, hotels, and bed-and-breakfast accommodations, many excellent restaurants for all tastes, including fast-food burger and pizza places, and plenty of gift and curio shops for the browser. In addition, there are U.S. Forest Service and private campgrounds all around the lake, along with a number of RV parks.

LAKE GREGORY

SPECIES: Rainbow and brown trout, crappies, bass.
BEST TIME: April through October.
FLIES: Imitations of damselfly nymphs, Woolly Buggers, Woolly Worms, and the occasional dry fly. An Adams will work nearly all the time.

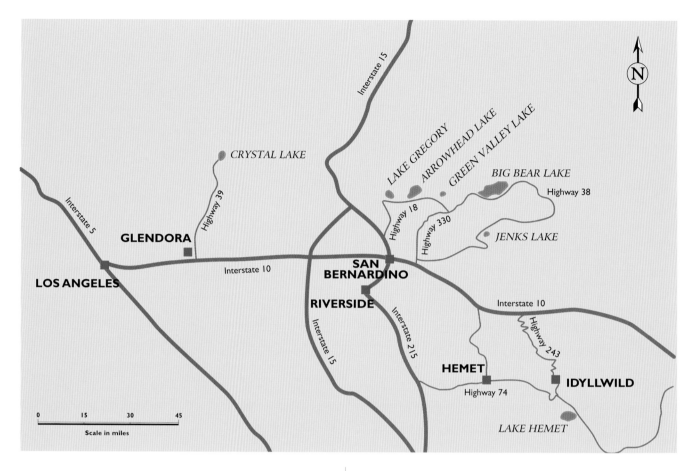

FLOAT TUBES: Yes, but you must put in at the boathouse, rather than at other spots on the lake. Rental boats are available. There is no private motorboat launch, but you can launch a private sailboat or bring an electric motor for a rental boat.

LOCATION: In Crestline in the San Bernardino Mountains. Lake Gregory is 70 miles east of Los Angeles. Take Highway 18 from San Bernardino. It is 14 miles to the lake.

Lake Gregory is both a beautiful small lake in a mountain setting and a highly developed recreation lake for both mountain residents and hordes of tourists during the summer months. It is just 120 surface acres and can get a bit crowded on summer weekends. In addition to fishing, there are small sailboats, paddleboards, and aquacycles on the lake at times.

On the other hand, Gregory gets a fair number of fly anglers who float tube the lake to get at some quite decent-sized trout. The state and the county both stock rainbow trout from April through October. The lake's elevation is 4,520 feet, and the water is cold enough for trout year around. The Department of Fish and Game stocks the normal range of planter rainbows, but the county also purchases trout from the Whitewater Hatchery. These are plump, well-conditioned trout, somewhat larger than the state's fish, and at times you may find big broodstock fish in the mix. It's not all that rare to see rainbows of 5 or 6 pounds cruising the weed beds.

The other fish of major interest is the brown trout. These were stocked some years ago as fingerlings. There have been mixed results from this attempt to create a fishery. The browns were stocked not just to provide variety, but to grow big enough to tackle an ongoing problem at Gregory: the stunted crappies that swarm the shallows. It's possible to catch a crappie every cast for as many casts as you can make. Any small fly that hits the water is a goner, but the fish you get are not going to be much bigger than the palm of your hand.

The brown trout, it was thought, would grow by feeding on the small crappies, making a good fishery for both species by weeding out the surplus crappies and turning them into trout flesh on the browns. The remaining crappies also would benefit, and larger crappies should result. The program is only a few years old, and so far (as of 1999), results are minimal. Not many anglers are catching browns, although I'm told a 3-pound-plus brown has been caught. Most people think the fish haven't survived. Not so, say the DFG biologists I talked to. The browns probably are still there, eating crappies and growing. They think the real story is that people just haven't figured out their habits at Lake Gregory, and the biologists still are hopeful the stocked browns will develop into a popular fishery.

Gregory is one of the few small lakes in the Southern California mountains that allows float tubes. (In addition to Big Bear, see Cuyamaca Reservoir and Lake Morena in Chapter 7.) The only drawback is that they want you to launch only at the boathouse. Because the lake is so small, this isn't a major prob-

Dawn at Lake Hemet sees a lone fly angler casting from the shore-line of his camp site.

lem, but at the time of this writing I was advised by manager Bart Ryder that the lake's managers have been considering creating a season pass for float-tube anglers and allowing pass holders to launch where they please.

In the summer, Gregory develops some serious weed beds, and fishing the outside edges of these during low-light periods is rewarding. The deeper water toward the middle of the lake is ideal for backtrolling a fly on a sinking line, and the area where the water aeration takes place attracts trout in the warmer weather. It should be no surprise that Gregory has a few largemouth bass, and some anglers have specialized in catching them. I doubt you'll find a bass much over 5 pounds, but you never know. The lake is open from the last Saturday in April to the last Sunday in October from 7:00 A.M. to 5:00 P.M. daily and opens at 6:00 A.M. on weekends. After the lake closes, however, you can still fish from the shore in a number of locations, a few of which are open enough for a decent backcast.

Because Lake Gregory is in "downtown" Crestline, all services, from gasoline to lodging and food are available within minutes. For more information, call the Lake Gregory office at (909) 338-2233.

LAKE HEMET

SPECIES: Rainbow trout, largemouth bass, and bluegills.
BEST TIME: Open year-round, but best from April through October.
FLIES: Weighted streamers and Woolly Buggers for bass. Dark dry flies in the smaller sizes work well, as do damselfly and dragonfly nymph imitations.
FLOAT TUBES: No. Private boats are allowed, and rental boats are permitted, plus there is good shore access on the north side, in the "Government Strip" area.
LOCATION: Lake Hemet is roughly 100 miles east of Los Angeles. Take Highway 74 from Hemet up the mountain to Mountain Center, then go east to the lake. You also can reach the lake from Interstate 10 at Banning via Highway 243 through Idyllwild to Mountain Center. It's a beautiful, if slow drive.

The only lake of any consequence on Mount San Jacinto in Riverside County, Lake Hemet is a water-storage reservoir of 420 surface acres. It lies in the scenic Garner Valley, not far from the town of Idyllwild. Unlike Lake Gregory, which is a put-and-take trout fishery that incidentally has some bass, Hemet is a put-and-take trout lake with real potential for the bass fly-rod enthusiast.

Hemet is open to angling year-round, and barring the occasional severe winter storm, the lake is fishable nearly every day. It's at 4,300 feet, so it gets cold enough to be tough to fish in winter, and warm enough on a summer day to make you want to limit fishing to the morning and the evening. Although private and rental boats are permitted, float tubes, canoes, and rafts are not allowed, nor is wading. There also are no personal watercraft or water skiers to contend with, a feature that will bring joy to many Southern California fly anglers.

The south side of the lake is not open to foot traffic, but because of an old mitigation agreement, there is a considerable stretch of land on the north side called the "Government Strip" where you can park in paved parking lots and walk to the water easily. This section was a no-fee area, with only a fishing license required until 1997, when the Forest Service implemented the Adventure Pass, the $5.00 daily or $30.00 annual use fee for all the national forests in Southern California.

This lake often is crowded with bait anglers during summer weekends, but is a great place to walk and fish on a weekday, particularly in the evenings. The shore is rocky, with huge boulders and weed beds that hold both trout and bass. It's also good to very good as a bluegill fishery. I've spent many evenings prowling with a 5-weight rod and some small poppers or rubber-leg foam spiders. Some really respectable bluegills have thumped a small bug dropped in pockets in the weeds or alongside a protruding rock.

It isn't always a bluegill, either. I have caught both trout and bass this way, and a couple of the bass that made heart-stopping boils on my little poppers weighed over 4 pounds. One spring evening, my wife and I fished the strip and caught bunches of 12-inch bass, hand-sized bluegills, and several planter trout, including one dandy holdover fish of 15 inches. If you camp in Lake Hemet's large public campground, you have shore access to more of the north side, and the summer weed beds hold a lot of small bass and bluegills there, as well.

For the boat angler, Hemet's western portion, from the Government Strip down past the dam and around to the south, is remarkable bass water. The whole area is filled with drowned brush, dead trees, and enormous rock formations. Fishing quality is dependent on the water level.

Like all reservoirs, Hemet is subject to drawdowns and the vagaries of winter rain and snow. When the water level is up, this part of the lake is great bass-bugging country in the early morning, but the smart bassing fly rodder will put away the bugging rod and switch to sinking lines and large streamers by midmorning on most days. The primary forage base is bluegills, rather than shad, so your choice of patterns should reflect that.

The trout fishing is interesting for a put-and-take fishery. The state plants on a regular schedule in the warmer months, but plants at odd intervals in the winter, as well, so there are fair numbers of holdover fish each spring. Hemet is fertile, and you see a number of really decent fish in the spring. Some anglers take trout in the 3-to-5-pound range in deeper water. Drifting in the main center channel of the lake with streamers or Woolly Buggers and full-sinking lines can produce interesting results.

You can find some hatching midges in the evenings. You can practically smother in them at times, and if the wind is still, dry-fly fishing is fair with small, dark, flies. Damselflies and dragonflies are very common. Nymphs of both types are a staple, and you also will find fair hatches of stillwater mayflies, but the exact imitation of anything is by no means mandatory.

Hemet is a lake where taking a couple of fish for the pan is an excellent idea. The holdover fish are pink and firm, and you are not hurting a thing by removing a few trout and bluegills from the lake. If your gastronomic interests run more to restaurant food on fishing trips, Idyllwild has a number of good places to eat, plus the sorts of stores, gift shops, and lodging facilities that one finds in most mountain recreation-area towns.

If you launch your own boat or rent one, there is a $7.00 daily use fee. The Hemet Lake Campground is huge, having around 1,000 dry camp sites for $11.50 per day per car and 166 sites with electricity, plus 160 with sewers. There are a lot of long-time campers who stay year-round, and the camp has daily, weekly, and monthly rates. For information, call (909) 659-2680.

OTHER MOUNTAIN LAKES

There are several small waters that might appeal to fly anglers in search of a bit of privacy or a casual fishing experience. Or in the case of Lake Arrowhead, a touch of class—the upper class. Arrowhead is a decent-sized mountain reservoir located east of Lake Gregory. Covering 740 surface acres, it is the kind of lake that looks good on postcards, and multimillion-dollar mansions surround the shore. Arrowhead has a fine trout fishery that includes some excellent angling for brown trout plus planted rainbows. There is also a good smallmouth bass fishery, and I have caught some very large crappies here. The lake is unusually clear, and in the summer, you can look down twenty feet or so and watch fish cruise over brilliant green weed beds.

Unless you know somebody, however, your chances of fishing Arrowhead are essentially nil. There's almost no access, you can't launch or rent a boat, and unless you're a homeowner or the friend of one, you aren't going to fish this lake. I've been lucky to fish it a couple of times, and the only advice I can give you is that you should make an effort to be pleasant to any homeowner you should happen to meet socially.

Green Valley Lake, several miles east of Arrowhead along Highway 18, is a very small reservoir of just twenty acres at 7,200 feet. It gets regular stocks of trout and is one of the few waters in the lower end of the state that has experimented with pen-raised trout, fish delivered from suppliers and raised to the proper release size in pens floating in the lake itself. The lake is open from the spring through the fall, and its managers charge a fishing fee. I'd tell you what it is, but they keep changing it. There are a few services locally, and campsites and lodging can be found nearby. For more information, call (909) 867-2009.

Even smaller is Jenks Lake, a 5-acre pond that has picnic facilities. You must pay a $5.00 parking fee, plus have a state license if you plan on fishing. I mention this lake only because it is located in the same general area of Barton Flats on Highway 38 that gains you access to Bear Creek and the Santa Ana River. (See Chapter 3.) It gets plants of catchable trout from the spring through the fall and is a fair place to take a beginner for a first stillwater outing. Crystal Lake in the Angeles National Forest off Highway 39, some 27 miles north of Azusa, is similar. It is 7 acres and has trout and some bluegills. These are essentially picnic areas, though, rather than real fisheries.

In addition to Chapter 7's descriptions of Cuyamaca Reservoir and Lake Morena in San Diego County, anglers also should see Chapter 6 for a description of Silverwood Lake in San Bernardino County. These three are at high enough altitudes that they might have been included here, but they are unique fisheries that deserve separate treatment.

CHAPTER FIVE

BASS AND TROUT LAKES IN THE L.A. BASIN

DESPITE THE PACE OF LIFE IN AND AROUND LOS Angeles, there are places relatively nearby where the contemplative angler can enjoy a bit of respite while casting a line. Of course, because this is Southern California, he or she may have to struggle through a crowd to reach the water and duck the more than an occasional personal watercraft ridden by a manners-challenged adolescent. Still, there are a number of lakes, ponds, and reservoirs that offer the opportunity for fishing for both warmwater and coldwater species. Most have resident populations of largemouth bass, bluegills, redear sunfish, and crappies, and add trout a on a put-and-take basis during the winter months, when water temperatures permit.

Some lakes cater to fly anglers to one degree or another, but at a few you are simply on your own among the nightcrawler and scented-cheese crowd. This isn't necessarily bad, however. There are times when a fly properly fished will outproduce everything else, which can be a great boost to your ego. You might convert a couple of bait anglers to the fly, as well.

In the Los Angeles basin, the giant valley that stretches from the beaches of the Pacific in the west to Riverside and San Bernardino Counties in the east, and from the Angeles National Forest in the north to the southern end of Orange County's suburban sprawl, most of the lakes are operated by the state park system or various county parks. A few are city-owned (See Chapter 2). A small number are privately operated. All offer trout fishing during the winter months that ranges from fair to good, and several offer outstanding warmwater action during the rest of the year.

If the idea of tossing flies at put-and-take trout is less than inspiring, let me point out that the height of this pay-to-play trout fishing occurs during the months when the lakes and streams in the eastern Sierra are closed and fly anglers in other parts of the country are stuck tying flies and reading books. You, on the other hand, may spend a weekend casting to rainbow or brown trout weighing several pounds or more, and doing it in shorts and a T-shirt in January!

IRVINE LAKE

SPECIES: Rainbow and brown trout, largemouth bass, bluegills, and crappies.

BEST TIME: For trout, from November to May. For bass and panfish, from March to November.

FLIES: Woolly Buggers, beadhead nymphs, and small streamers that match threadfin shad and small minnows.

FLOAT TUBES: Yes, on Monday, Wednesday, and Friday. Also private boats are allowed, and rental boats are available.

LOCATION: Irvine Lake is east of the city of Orange. From the 91 Free-

Barbara Bean with a fine rainbow from Irvine Lake. This big fish hooked itself so deeply it had to be kept—not a problem with stocked trout. It made a great meal.

way, take the Newport Freeway (55) south to Chapman Avenue. Or take Interstate 5 to the Garden Grove Freeway (22), head east to the Newport Freeway, then go north to Chapman Avenue. From Chapman Avenue, go east to Santiago Canyon Road, then turn right and follow it to the lake. It's about 8 miles from the Newport Freeway to the lake.

Irvine Lake is what some would term a "pay-to-play" lake. A state fishing license is not required, but the lake charges a fee for providing eager anglers with plenty of trout in the winter and equal amounts of catfish during the summer. It also supports a better than average catch-and-release fishery for largemouth bass and encourages float-tube anglers. A 660-surface-acre reservoir lying in the rolling foothills of suburban Orange County, it's only a few miles from some of the most densely populated areas in the state, but it manages to provide a respite from the daily grind and some more than decent fishing, as well.

Although mornings may be chilly, and the coastal fog often blankets the lake, the midday sun at Irvine on any warm weekend usually reveals fishermen laid back in folding lounge chairs behind their rod holders, dressed in tank tops and shorts, even during January. Fly anglers plying their trade from the comfortable confines of a float tube may need chest waders to insulate them from the water's chill, but they may long for a short-sleeved shirt by noon.

Formerly known as Santiago Canyon Reservoir, Irvine is a Y-shaped body of water with a mix of both shallows and deeper water. The shallows have brush and stickups for panfish and largemouth bass, and the deeper water harbors trout and giant catfish. For many years, Irvine Lake's claim to fame has been the extensive stocking of trout in the winter, when the lake management stops stocking catfish and begins releasing hordes of rainbow trout into the cooling waters of this lowland reservoir.

"The trout season at Irvine runs from the first week or so of November all the way into June in most years," said Jim Niemiec, the former lake manager at Irvine. In addition to being capable with conventional tackle, he is a fly angler.

Because aquatic recreation in Southern California has to compete with other recreational interests, lakes like Irvine get involved in games of one-upsmanship with other nearby waters, leading to lots of promotion and the stocking of some amazing trout. "In a typical year, Irvine will stock until they've put 175,000 pounds of trout in the lake," Niemiec said. "All of the trout will be of catchable size. There will probably be no trout stocked under 10 pounds, there will be trout up to perhaps 17 or18 pounds, and there will be numerous fish in the 5- to 8-pound class."

I have fished Irvine on and off for a number of years, catching a few large trout, and I have been there when some real monster brood-stock trout have been caught. What's surprising is that these big fish from private hatcheries are not the dummies you might expect. Pen-raised they may be, but they can be incred-

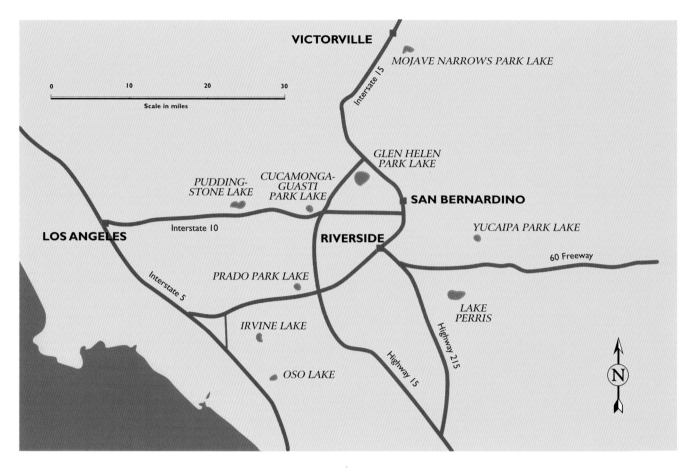

ibly wary, and refined tackle with long, tapered leaders is necessary to really score on the biggest fish.

Niemiec noted that Irvine's water conditions generally are very good in the winter. The lake has an aeration system that keeps the water stirred, so there's very little oxygen-related stratification. The water temperatures stay nearly constant from top to bottom throughout much of the lake, and that should mean that trout can be found at all depths—except for one thing.

"One hot tip I can tell you is that Mount Lassen Farms, where we get our trout, raises their fish in shallow ponds," Niemiec noted. "When the trout get stocked in Irvine, they tend to seek out similar conditions, so they head for shallow water. They like the sandy shoreline that duplicates the ponds they were raised in."

This sandy shore is mostly along the west side of Irvine, an area with a gentle slope that makes it ideal for the trout—and there's good access for anglers, as well. In the winter, when the water levels are down some, there can be as much as a couple of miles of shore line that's readily accessible.

"Boat anglers can fish anywhere, of course, but I think they will do best if they position their boat and cast toward the shore and retrieve through the shallows," Niemiec volunteered.

"If you find a section of sandy beach where you aren't interfering with the shore fishermen, you can score by moving fairly close to the beach. Most of the strikes you get will come in less than 10 feet of water."

Niemiec also noted that during warmer weather, the fish move into deeper areas between the shoreline and Rocky Point, near the dam end of the lake. When this migration occurs, conventional-tackle anglers can catch significant numbers of trout by fishing deep with lead-core lines or downriggers—or by soaking bait deep. The fish do move around, however, and you might catch a few in shallow water in the summer, but the most practical technique would be backtrolling in a float tube or drifting with a boat and electric trolling motor while fishing with deep-sinking lines to get a fly down into the strike zone.

The bass fishing can be very interesting. The late spring and summer offer top-water angling that ranges from good to very good. Early in the spring, you may find bass back in Santiago Flats and hanging along the edge of the creek channel on the north side of the lake, but I've had good luck just walking the bank and casting a Marabou Muddler to brush in the South Fork and West Fork coves. Float tubes give you an edge, and you should investigate man-made structure, such as docks, and give Sierra Cove a try, as well. In the fall, you can find the bass crashing baitfish in open water, and don't be surprised if a cork popper, properly placed, gets inhaled by a very large bass.

All the bass fishing at Irvine is catch-and-release. This might surprise some fly fishers, but largemouth bass are extremely popular, and because it is not economically feasible to restock them (growth rates and the amount of food required to raise bass to catchable size are the problems), the lake has taken the step of managing the bass fishery for self-sustaining angling. Bass spawn naturally in lakes, unlike trout, and this is a wise step that other lakes in the area might imitate.

Irvine Lake is open seven days a week. Hours are 6:00 A.M. to 7:00 P.M. on weekdays and until 11:00 P.M. on Fridays and Saturdays in the summer at no extra charge. No California state fishing license is required to fish Irvine, but there is a daily fishing fee of $13.00 for adults, $10.00 for seniors, and $7.00 for children aged four to twelve. Boat rentals are $40.00 on weekends, $25.00 on weekdays. Rowboats are $25.00 on weekends and $20.00 on weekdays for those who have their own motors. Rentals of fishing pontoon boats are $85.00. Patio boats are $100. Anglers may launch their own boats for an $8.00 fee, $6.00 for seniors. There's no motor size restriction, but there is a 5-mile-per-hour speed limit. Float-tube fishing is allowed with a $3.00 launch fee.

The lake has a store and tackle shop with most of the things conventional-tackle anglers need, plus food and drink. The daily limits are 5 trout and 10 panfish. As I said, bass fishing is catch-and-release only. For fly tackle and information, check with Mike Scott's at 2324 N. Batavia Street, Suite 116, Orange, CA 92865, (714) 998-9400 or Bob Marriott's Fly Fishing Store, 2700 W. Orangethorpe Avenue, Fullerton, CA 92833, (714) 525-1827. For more information, call the recorded hot line at (949) 460-4940 or the lake office at (949) 649-9111. The lake has a web site at www.fishinghotpage.com/irvine.

OSO LAKE

SPECIES: Northern-strain and Florida-strain largemouth bass, plus panfish.
BEST TIME: Open year-round, but best during the spring and fall.
FLIES: Poppers and streamers. Anything large and ugly.
FLOAT TUBES: Yes. Also, private boats are allowed and rental boats are available. Electric motors only.
LOCATION: Orange County. Take Interstate 5 to El Toro, then go northeast on El Toro Road about 7 miles until you see a sign that says "Oso Fishing Assoc." Turn right and follow the road to the gate.

Oso Lake is similar in some respects to other Los Angeles basin bass lakes, but it has one definite difference. Oso is managed as a private lake with an annual fee for Oso Sportsmen's Organization members. Oso also is open to anglers who aren't club members, but it charges the general public a higher fee than either of the other pay-to-play lakes. What you get in return, however, is less angler pressure and a more inviting atmosphere than the more crowded waters.

Oso is smaller than the more popular Irvine Lake, with just 130 surface acres, but the lower density of anglers makes it seem larger than it actually is. Built in 1976 by a local water company, Oso was stocked, but not fished (except by a few poachers) until 1988, when the Oso Sportsmen's Organization obtained fishing rights to the reservoir. Also managed as a catch-and-release bass fishery, Oso has a lake record of 16 pounds, 4 ounces, but anglers find the average bass more like 2 to 3 pounds, with enough 6-to-8-pound fish lurking in the weed beds to keep

things very interesting. The lake has all kinds of structure and vegetation, making it a natural bass pond.

"As a matter of fact, we've had to selectively harvest for the past couple of years, and because of that, we are seeing more bass in the 4-to-7-pound range now," said consulting biologist Ray Diaz. "We've removed about 2 to 3 pounds of fish per acre of 10-to-14-inch fish. It took about one season to see some results. We are seeing some larger fish now. And the real thing is that we see fewer fish with parasites or other health problems." Diaz also noted that the bass had reduced the bluegill population and said that they stocked about 50 bluegills per acre back into the lake, and that's had a beneficial impact.

"The fishing is quite good. It's something like 15 to 20 fish per day, on artificials only—no live bait." Diaz said. "I think anything that mimics a shad is best. Fly fishermen love Oso. When the water is up, they crowd into the bushes and get 40 to 50 fish per day."

In addition to shad patterns, large poppers will produce hits, and you might try the biggest Marabou Muddler or other bulky marabou fly you have. Local angler Harry Smith has produced flies that look like a baby bird and has fished them in the half-flooded treetops and brush with great success. Frog flies with wiggly rubber legs also are a good bet. This is one lake that probably requires a floating line more than a sinking one, and the clear waters favor long, but not light leaders for most fishing.

When asked to compare the lake with other suburban waters, Diaz said he would rate Oso as an excellent suburban fishery. "Because it's privately operated, they can keep the numbers of anglers matched to the fishery. We don't really limit the anglers, it's just that you just don't see that many each day except for the early spring. Lots of guys float tube Oso. It's all electric motors for the boat anglers. It's a great, peaceful getaway right in the middle of Orange County."

That, of course, is what makes Oso popular with many anglers. It no longer is in the middle of nowhere—constant building in Orange County has seen to that—but it has enough wild spaces and enough water to serve as a true refuge from the hustle and bustle for the limited number of anglers who fish it.

Annual membership in the Oso Sportsmen's Organization is $500.00, and each member has to agree to take 10 kids under the age of 14 fishing at least once a year. Guests over 14 are $20.00 per day, and kids under 14 are free. Teen guests aged 15 to 19 cost $10.00. Public anglers are welcome. The daily fee is $40.00. You can rent a boat with an electric motor for $30.00 or a rowboat for $15.00. As noted, bass fishing is catch-and-release, but Oso has no limit on catfish, and bluegills are plentiful.

Oso is open every day except Tuesdays and Thanksgiving, Christmas, and New Years days. For more information, call (949) 858-9313 or write to the Oso Sportsmen's Organization, 19387 Live Oak Canyon Road, Trabuco, CA 92679.

LAKE PERRIS

SPECIES: Rainbow trout, largemouth and spotted bass, bluegills, and redear sunfish.

BEST TIME: November through June.

FLIES: For bass, large shad patterns and crayfish imitations. For Florida-strain bluegills, try beadhead nymphs in olive or black, Woolly Buggers, and rubber-leg designs such as the Bitch Creek Nymph. For trout, use damselfly nymphs, beadhead designs, Woolly Worms, or Woolly Buggers.

FLOAT TUBES: Yes. Wading also is permitted, and there are launch facilities for private boats. From April through October, however, you need reservations to launch a boat.

LOCATION: 70 miles east of Los Angeles and 80 miles north of San Diego. The lake has three entrances. The north and south gates normally are manned, and there's a unmanned pay-envelope gate on the east side of the lake. From Los Angeles, take the Pomona Freeway, (Highway 60) to Moreno Beach Drive, then go south to the northern entrance or turn south on 215E to the Ramona Expressway. It's about 3 miles to the southern entrance from there.

Lake Perris is one of my favorite stillwater fly-fishing spots in Southern California. It gets crowded at times, especially in midsummer, when you have to compete with hordes of boaters and skiers, but in the winter and spring, it offers excellent bass fishing and not only has a record-class bluegill fishery, but supports some fair to good winter trout angling as well.

Perris was an oddity to begin with. Hunkered down in what used to be a combination of desert and farmland on the west side of Southern California's Riverside County, Perris is a child of the quest for more and more water for urban expansion. A roughly triangular reservoir of 2,300 surface acres, Perris is part of the California Water Project and is operated as a recreation site by the California State Park system.

Perris opened for recreation and fishing in 1974 and was selected by the California Department of Fish and Game for an experiment in establishing a fishery for the Alabama spotted bass, a subspecies that shares some of the physical features of both largemouth and smallmouth bass. A newspaper account of the bass fishing in Perris written in 1976 noted Lake Perris was decided on because it was a new lake with no predators bigger than the spotted bass, and since there were no other bass, there was no danger of hybridization. The article didn't mention that the spotted bass fishery might be threatened or even destroyed in the future by problems not anticipated by biologists.

At first, the experiment worked well. Ninety-five spotted bass brought from Alabama spawned quickly, and in a few years, anglers were catching "spots" weighing from 3 to 5 pounds. There was every evidence that Perris would produce even better results. This began to happen by the late 1970s. A 9-

R. G. Fann displays a largemouth bass caught in the shallows of Lake Perris. During spring, the easily-wadeable eastern shoreline can provide exciting top-water action for the fly angler.

pound, 2-ounce spot was caught in 1979. This was larger than the 8-pound, 10-ounce record current then, although the angler didn't realize the fish was a record until too late. And in 1982, a flurry of 7-pound and 8-pound spotted bass were hooked by happy anglers.

But then the growth of the fishery began to splutter like a car running out of gas, seeming to die, then roaring to life. In 1984, a 9-pound, 1-ounce football-shaped spot was caught and weighed in by Jeff Matthews of Redlands for a new state and International Game Fish Association world record, but not many other big spotted bass were caught. Then, in 1987, the spotted bass fishing at Perris again came to life with a flurry of giant spotted bass being taken, including a double world record for the species at 9 pounds, 4 ounces, held by Gil Rowe and Steve West, two Southern California anglers. Steve West's huge bass was caught on January 24, 1987, and Gil Rowe's equally bulky bass came on April 1, 1987. Perris finally lost the world record to Pine Flat Lake when Coalinga angler Bob Shelton caught a 9-pound, 7-ounce spotted bass there, but the IGFA still shows that in its 7 spotted bass line classes, Lake Perris is the home of 5.

Not many lakes can lay claim to producing two world record fish within three months of each other. Sadly for local anglers, however, this once fine spotted bass fishery is in decline. The exact cause is uncertain, but most experts think it was the introduction of Florida-strain largemouths, possibly from nearby Vail Lake (now closed to the public) or one of the San Diego Bass lakes. Biologists and anglers alike believe that the largemouths simply out-competed the spotted bass for food and spawning areas.

It is hard to get most anglers worked up over the decline of the spotted bass fishery, however, because the illegal introduction of largemouth bass again put Perris in contention as one of the bass lakes with record-setting potential. You may encounter spotted bass still, and some can be of good size, from 3 to 6 pounds, but their numbers are dwindling.

"With the [illegal] introduction of the largemouth, Perris is a changed lake," said DFG lakes biologist Terry Foreman. "We are going to retain the 2-fish, 15-inch limit. We thought about putting the reg back to the 5-fish, 12-inch limit, but decided against it." That's good news for the largemouths and for the catch-and-release angler. A great early-spring fishery, Perris is noted for good fish coming to conventional-tackle anglers on live crayfish and jigs. Some spectacular catches also have come to anglers throwing big trout-shaped lures just after a stocking.

That is a key for the fly angler. Matching the hatch at Perris means fishing crayfish and minnow patterns. Threadfin shad, shiners, trout, and baby bluegills all get consumed by bass, and this gives the fly tier a wide range of shapes, sizes, and colors to imitate. Although you can fall back on some of the simple attractor patterns such as the Woolly Worm and Woolly Bugger and do well, it never hurts to let your penchant for invention run a bit beyond the everyday.

Variations on the Wiggle Craw and other crayfish patterns

fished on full-sinking lines will catch some large fish, as will silvery-white shad streamers. Local guide and fly expert Bob Slamal finds that drifting along the face of the dam with a full-sinking line and a shad pattern is a dynamite way to take bass in the summer months.

The thing that gets most fly anglers going, however, is the spring bass fishing in the upper, northeastern end of the lake. Much of the eastern shore, from the Bernasconi Beach entrance around to the point where the water slide is located, is filled with brush and trees that provide dense cover for bass and bait. When lake levels are up, this area is easily wadeable, or you can float tube it. In most Southern California lakes, sinking lines are the primary method of getting flies to the fish, but Perris in the spring is almost strictly floating-line country.

If the spring is warm and dry, topwater action typically begins in March. By April of any year, however, you'll find anglers stalking like herons through the brush, sight casting to cruising bass that may go anywhere from a pound to dark, torpedo-shaped shadows that may reach 10 pounds or more. The Perris lake record for largemouth bass is nearly 17 pounds, so you should be aware that any cast could produce the biggest bass of your life.

The shallow-water fishing can extend into May, but by then, most of the larger fish have slipped back into deeper water. The spawn is over, and the constant boat and personal-watercraft traffic is more than they can handle. June, however, can see a surprising resumption of feeding activity at or near the surface. This can occur both in the shallows and over deep water as the bass drive bait to the surface in feeding sprees. Perris, and indeed most of the Los Angeles basin, often is foggy and overcast. Weather people refer to the pattern as the "June Gloom." Foggy days are good for fishing, and an early morning bike ride on the paved path to the back side of the lake with your float tube gets you to good fishing in just a few minutes.

Summer bass fishing at Perris, in July, August, and September, often is not worth the effort for the fly angler. Summer is party time at Perris for boaters, skiers, and personal-watercraft riders. The traffic situation is such that from April to October, you need a reservation to put a boat on the water, and for the fly angler, the hoopla is almost too much.

The spring and summer are good times to target panfish, however. Perris has two excellent panfish, the redear sunfish and the bluegill. Redears reach respectable size, but can be hard to catch unless you like to drag the bottom with sinking lines. The bluegills in Perris are another story altogether. They were originally transplanted from Florida, and like Florida-strain largemouth bass, they grow to enormous size. The lake record is near the 4-pound mark, and it's not uncommon to catch bluegills in the 2-pound range. The east side and the area around the marina often are the best places. Evening fishing with a small cork popper can leave you breathless when a 2-pound-plus bluegill strikes with the force of a striper eating a shad.

Once the weather cools in the fall, anglers get more breathing room and can concentrate on the submerged rock piles and the artificial reefs made of tires on the east side of the lake near Bernasconi Beach. The long, curving dam with two miles of craggy riprap is another excellent area, as are the riprap points around the launch ramps. There are some closures on the east side during the waterfowl hunting season, but this doesn't limit much of the fishing.

Once water temperatures dip into the fifties, the state begins stocking rainbow trout. The west end of the dam is a hot spot, as are the riprap points around the launch ramps. As an added benefit, some very large bass show up to hunt the confused planters at each stocking, and anglers equipped with large streamers that look like trout just might be in for the battle of their lives if they should be there within a day of the plant.

Fishing for the trout themselves is fairly straightforward. Small, simple attractor patterns and nymphs probably work best. A sinking or sink-tip line and a long, light leader will work around the launch ramp and off the points between the marina and launch area. As the trout move deeper and spread out into the lake, a quick-sink shooting head designed to get a fly down from 10 to 20 feet or more, fished near the west end of the dam, probably is the best bet.

At just over 1,500 feet in altitude and 2,370 surface acres, Perris is an ideal winter fishery, with a mild climate most of the year. It's quite hot during the summer, and can be cold and frequently windy in winter. The lake is open year around, with park hours running from 6:00 A.M. to 8:00 P.M. in the winter and 6:00 A.M. to 10:00 P.M. during the summer.

The day use fee is $6.00 per car, and boat launching is an additional $5.00 per vessel. The lake has a full-service marina with boat rentals and excellent launch ramps. Call (909) 657-2179. There also are bait-and-tackle shops and snack-bar facilities.

Tent camping during the winter months is $14.00. RV sites are $18.00. The summer season runs from Memorial Day to Labor Day. Campground, boating, and day-use reservations can be made by calling 1-800-444-7275. Boat reservations are taken all year. Because of the summer crowds, they are needed seven days a week during the summer season and on weekends during the winter. For additional information, call the park office at (909) 657-0676.

PUDDINGSTONE RESERVOIR

SPECIES: Largemouth bass, rainbow trout, bluegills, and redear sunfish.
BEST TIME: October through June.
FLIES: Woolly Buggers, beadhead nymphs, and small streamers that match threadfin shad and small minnows.
FLOAT TUBES: No. Private boats are allowed, and rental boats are available, however There also is good shore access.
LOCATION: 30 miles east of Los Angles in Bonelli Regional Park, near the intersection of Interstate 10 and Interstate 210. Take I-10 to I-210 north, exit on Via Verde Avenue, then take Via Verde Park Road to the lake.

At about 250 surface acres in size, Puddingstone Lake clearly is in a different category from the tiny city and county ponds you find in most parks. It is inside Frank G. Bonelli Regional County Park on the northeastern corner of Pomona

and is operated by the Los Angeles Parks Department. In the summer, it gets a lot of high-speed boat traffic, including boat races on some weekends, not to mention personal watercraft on alternate days. In the winter, things are more relaxed, and that's when much of the best fishing occurs, as well.

The Department of Fish and Game plants catchable rainbow trout during the cooler months, and the county sometimes adds trout of its own during trout derbies. The lake has a sizeable population of bass and a forage base that includes threadfin shad, redear sunfish, bluegills and crayfish. The redears and bluegills constitute a great fishery in their own right. The lake record for bass is over 14 pounds, but anglers shouldn't expect to find lots of big fish, just fair numbers of fish and a few larger ones.

Puddingstone can be a bit of a sleeper. It gets pounded, but the pressure comes from recreational boaters and personal-watercraft operators, rather than from anglers. There's access to parking and fishing areas along nearly the entire shoreline, and it is one of those places better fished on a weekday, if you can manage it.

Many anglers remember fishing Puddingstone prior to the extensive development of the park, and I can still visualize parking near the control tower at nearby Brackett Field and ducking through the fence to make the long walk to the south side of the lake. In those days, there were no roads or vehicle

Steve Miller with an example of the trout stocked at several "pay-to-play" lakes in the Los Angeles basin. Although not wild, huge fish like this are surprisingly wary.

access, and sometimes you could fish the shoreline all day long without seeing anybody else unless they were in a boat. That's not likely to happen these days, but the lake is still a good spot for a few hours of angling. Wading and float-tube fishing are not allowed, but you can prowl the shore and cast to weed beds and rocky structure.

You'll likely hook quite a few small bass, which are fun on a light rod, but with a sinking line you could find yourself attached to something large and angry. One local lure manufacturer noted there's a lot of nice bass in Puddingstone, not lots of lunkers, but fair numbers of bass over 10 pounds, and lots of four-pound and five-pound fish. He told me he had seen a limit taken (and released) by a club tournament angler that totaled 21 pounds, 4 ounces for 5 fish. That included fish weighing 6 pounds, 8 ounces; 5 pounds, 1 ounce; 4 pounds, 8 ounces; 3 pounds, 12 ounces; and 1 pound, 7 ounces.

Anglers should split the lake into two sections. The portion to the east and south is good spring and summer water, while the deeper and steeper areas to the north and west are the better spots in winter. The extreme eastern end near the airport is flat and shallow. The west winds often blow schools of bait

into these shallows, and that creates some interesting top-water fishing. There are extensive clam beds off the main launch area, which also is a good spot for bass. This is also where the trout are stocked in winter.

The whole area near the rental boat dock is good for bass. Along the southwestern and southern shore there is decent bass and panfish habitat. Sailboat Cove and the point there (near the dam) also are worth checking out. The back of Sailboat Cove has some spots where bass spawn, and the center of the cove is quite deep. If you are in a boat with a depth finder, a number of submerged humps range outward from the point; these quite often bass. Beds of aquatic weeds beds ring much of the lake, and in the summer you'll often experience fine top-water fishing in the morning and evening.

Puddingstone has many services, including camping, and everything else can be obtained in the surrounding communities of San Dimas, La Verne, and Pomona. Bonelli Park is open 7 days a week, year around. Summer fishing hours are from sunrise to 10:00 P.M. for shore anglers. Winter hours run from sunrise to 7:00 P.M. The day use fee is $6.00 per car, and the boat launch fee also is $6.00. An annual combined auto and boat permit is $155.00. The speed limit on the lake is 35 miles per hour. For information on boat rentals, call (909) 599-2667. Boat owners should be aware that summer crowds require limiting the use of boats and personal watercraft to alternate days. Call ahead for a schedule at the park office, (909) 599-8411. A California fishing license is required. Limits are five bass, with a twelve-inch minimum length, five trout, and twenty-five crappies. There is no limit on bluegills and redear sunfish.

OTHER WATERS

A number of smaller lakes in the basin have fair to good bass, trout, and panfish action at one time of the year or another. Most of these were covered in Chapter 2 because they fall into the class of city and county park ponds stocked with trout by the Department of Fish and Game in its expanding Urban Fishing Program.

A few others come to mind. One is Corona Lake, a 30-surface-acre reservoir between the cities of Corona and Elsinore off Interstate 15 at Temescal Canyon Road. It contains hybrid striped bass, and so is covered in detail in Chapter 6, but Corona also has sizeable populations of largemouth bass and panfish, and gets planted with trout during the winter. A privately-operated fee lake, it has a considerable amount of submerged brush, and the upper end is full of trees. Float tubes are allowed, and fishing the dense tree line can produce some good action for bass and bluegills. For more information, see Chapter 6.

The lakes operated by the San Bernardino County Regional Park system have some potential for the fly angler. They are in Yucaipa, Glen Helen, Cucamonga-Guasti, Prado, and Mojave Narrows Regional Parks. All get plants of trout during the winter. Schedules and amounts vary. Usually it is a mix of catchable-sized fish from the DFG, plus larger county-supplied fish from the Whitewater Hatchery. In the summer, they switch to planting catfish, but all these lakes have at least some bass and panfish.

One in particular, Mojave Narrows Regional Park (actually located in Victorville, outside the L.A. basin), has a lovely pair of lakes ringed with trees and tules. Horseshoe Lake is the larger of the two, at about 20 acres, and Pelican Lake (which often has real pelicans on it) is about 10 acres. Both lakes have bass, bluegills, and some crappies. Horseshoe has a few really large bass. I've personally seen nesting female largemouths that weighed in excess of 10 pounds. They are difficult to catch, but a fly rod is a good tool. In my fishing life, I've caught two bass over the 9-pound mark. One of these came from Horeseshoe Lake a few years ago. For more information on all these lakes, call (909) 38-PARKS.

The lakes discussed in this chapter are not the only ones in the Los Angeles basin that have bass and/or trout seasonally, but the others that are not covered in other chapters because of their unique features are not suitable for fly fishing. The fishing at all these lakes is done primarily in the winter, spring, and fall. In the summer, you're better off fishing the trout streams and multiple-species lakes in the mountains that surround the Los Angeles basin at altitudes high enough to have adequately cool water temperatures.

Bob Slamal and Luc Paquet work the fertile waters of Lake Perris. They're fishing full-sink lines with small, dark flies. The boat's drift is controlled with a trolling motor.

CHAPTER SIX

STRIPER FEVER, SOUTHERN STYLE

ACCORDING TO THE REST OF AMERICA, EVERYTHING in California is a bit off-center. It could be they're right—at least that would be one reason why a fish from the chill, storm-tossed waters of the North Atlantic could be transplanted into lakes and rivers in California and quickly become accepted as a great "local" sport fish. Like the brown trout, also an import from Europe, the striped bass has gone native.

Originally from the Atlantic coast, where they are both a commercial catch and a sport fish in salt water, stripers were spread to the Pacific Ocean before the start of this century. They came by rail in a milk can as immigrants from the East to Pacific waters and were planted in the San Francisco Bay and Sacramento Delta areas in 1879.

They quickly became the basis of a major saltwater and estuary fishery. Starting with just 132 tiny stripers, the Pacific striper population ballooned to fantastic dimensions. Within twenty years of this first stocking (there were follow-on stocks at several spots), 1.2 million pounds of stripers per year were being removed from the Pacific by commercial fishing interests, and they were fast becoming a major component of the recreational fishery in the San Francisco area.

They might have stayed in Northern California, except for one important fact. While striped bass in their native habitat spend much of their lives in salt water, running salmonlike into fresh water to spawn, they can survive year-round in fresh water. This was discovered when striped bass were trapped in Southern river systems in the East as the great TVA dams of the 1930s were built. The stripers not only survived when isolated from their saltwater environment, they prospered, and within a few years were busting tackle and startling bass anglers all over the South.

In the days when biologists thought the striped bass could live, but not reproduce, in the conditions found in reservoirs and lakes, fishery managers considered landlocked stripers as the perfect stockable sport fish, and they were deliberately introduced into many lakes and river systems across the country. The fish, however, also began to show up in places they never were intended to be. Stripers migrating unbidden began giving fishery managers migraine headaches trying to manage an unmanageable species.

For once, California turned out to be no different from any other place. When the California Aqueduct was finished, bringing water from the Sacramento Delta to expansion-hungry Southern California cities, striped bass got into the system. Once sucked out of the Delta by the system's giant pumps, they made the trip to reservoirs in the Southland unassisted. Since then, they not only have provided an outstanding striper fishery in the entire length of the aqueduct, which starts at San Luis Reservoir and heads south over 400 miles to the Los Angeles area,

Bob Slamal with a fly-caught striper at Lake Skinner.

they also have invaded several reservoirs and established themselves as the biggest, worst-tempered fresh-water sport fish in Southern California.

In each of the waters that stripers have populated (some would say "infected"), they've aroused passion both for and against their presence. Voracious stripers consume anything they can catch. In waters they share with hatchery trout planted for put-and-take anglers, they've been accused of eating the majority of the stocked fish, to the delight of those anglers who use trout-shaped plugs to catch huge stripers and to the disgust of hatchery managers and trout fishermen, who think stripers ruin their fishing.

Bass anglers are equally against the striped bass. They feel the stripers compete with their cherished largemouth bass for food, eat young bass, and generally reduce the piscatorial monoculture most weekend bass anglers would like to see in each and every one of Southern California's lakes. The fact that largemouth bass also eat young largemouths, planted trout, and everything else they can get their cavernous mouth around escapes the tournament-fishing crowd. Love them or hate them, however, stripers appear to be here to stay.

For the fly angler, Southern California stripers offer a chance to cast flies to hard-fighting fish that grow to the kind of size and weight associated with tarpon or tuna. You can take a great "saltwater" trip on inland waters—stripers reside in the local reservoirs covered in this chapter, and they also roam the cool waters of the Colorado River, starting with giant Lakes Powell, Mead, Mohave, and Havasu (see Chapter 8). Castaic Lake has stripers, as well, although the largemouth bass fishery takes precedence there. For a description of Castaic, see Chapter 1.

Tackle for stripers is roughly the same you would select for largemouth bass. Six-weight to 9-weight rods, an array of floating and sinking lines, and streamer patterns that mimic the local baitfish are commonly used. It's hard to be more precise because stripers run from a few inches long to well over 50 pounds in some lakes. Typical fly-rod striped bass in Southern California might weigh from 3 to 4 pounds up to as much as 20 pounds.

You can catch striped bass on surface flies, but it's not a high-percentage method. A good-sized popper or skipping bug tossed into the feeding frenzy of a school of stripers mauling a ball of threadfin shad is likely to get the rod ripped out of your hands, but it doesn't happen nearly as often as a strike on a deep-fished streamer.

Stripers are not reticent about smacking something that moves quickly, and they definitely are not leader shy. With most 6-weight to 9-weight lines, a leader of 9 feet or shorter is fine, and tippets of 6 to 10 pounds test are not inappropriate. For sinking-line applications, a straight length of 6-pound or 8-pound test monofilament is as good as anything. I've had success

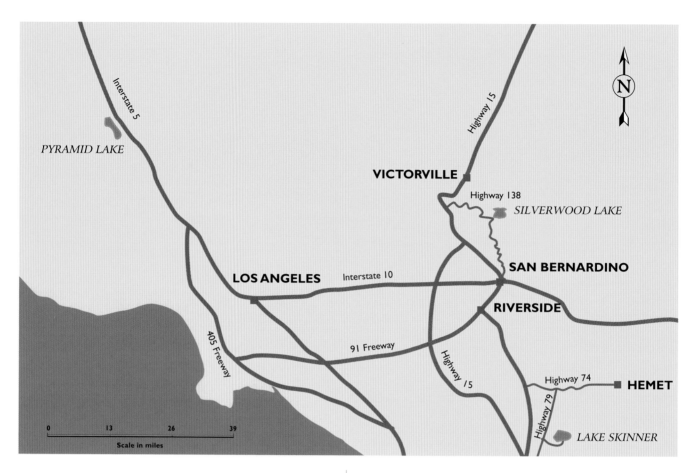

fishing leaders as short as 3 feet and as long as 10 feet, but anything sensible works.

Stripers can be choosy about the size of the prey they expect, so a reasonable selection of flies includes baitfish imitations from perhaps as short as 2 inches to as long as 7 or 8 inches if you are fishing just after a plant of hatchery trout. Simple streamers with a lot of white and some silver in the body and tail will work on stripers taking shad, and since striped bass will eat anything they can catch (they've been known to grub around eating freshwater clams and other bottom fodder, and they hunt crayfish, just like largemouth bass), your flies can replicate everything from baby bluegills, carp, crappies, several species of shiners, small bass, and of course, rainbow trout.

As for fly patterns, Lefty's Deceivers, Dan Blanton's Sar-Mul-Macs, large Clouser Minnows, and any number of saltwater flies will do a good job. Bob Slamal of Riverside guides for striped bass on Lake Skinner and uses a simple marabou streamer that looks a lot like a big Woolly Bugger, but tied with a marabou wing and using J. Fair's pearlescent shuck material as a body. It doesn't look like a shad to me, but the stripers think it's quite a good likeness and take it with a vengeance.

Many years ago, a pioneering striped bass fly-fishing couple, Dave and Freddie Cox, caught some mighty fish on the Colorado River using a white bucktail fly that was simplicity itself. The pattern was just a big bunch of white bucktail about 2 or 3 inches long tied on a 2/0 Mustad 3407 saltwater hook. It still is a highly

effective fly, and you can tie in large numbers in an evening. Compared with marabou or some of the synthetic materials, pure bucktail doesn't have a lot of flash or movement, but if you flare the hair around the hook shank, it will pulse open and closed with each strip of the line and give a pretty good imitation of something alive. I personally favor eyes on all my streamer flies, but this is one pattern that doesn't seem to need them

Striped bass will overrun a lake if their numbers are not kept in check as a result of regular predation by something bigger and hungrier than they are. The state regulations were amended in the early 1990s to increase the striped bass limit in a number of reservoirs from 2 fish, with a minimum size of 18 inches, to 10 fish, with no size limit. This regulation applies to the entire Southern District, which includes all the striped bass waters in this guide.

In Lake Skinner, tiny striped bass by the thousands school, and bait anglers are encouraged to take home a limit every time they fish. Department of Fish and Game biologist Mike Giusti told me he didn't think anglers could wipe out the stripers in Skinner if they tried. Still, most fly anglers release most or all of the stripers they catch, and a large number of the conventional-tackle striper anglers release big fish over the twenty-pound mark, keeping only a couple of smaller fish for the table.

That's an approach I agree with for all Southern California striped bass waters. Once they reach 10 pounds or so, stripers are immune to ordinary threats, and a sensible idea is to release the larger fish that might reach true trophy size. But please do take home more than a few of the medium-sized striped bass you catch. I'm probably biased, but I think striped bass are possibly the most flavorful fish you can put on a plate.

PYRAMID LAKE

SPECIES: Striped bass, largemouth and smallmouth bass, crappies, and bluegills.
BEST TIME: Stripers are most active from midsummer through November.
FLIES: Streamers that mimic threadfin shad. White and white with chartreuse are popular.
FLOAT TUBES: Yes, but a motorboat is necessary to reach most of the good areas.
LOCATION: 60 miles north of Los Angeles on Interstate 5. Take the Hungry Valley offramp, go to the west side of I-5 and take old Highway 99 south to the lake entrance.

Southern California's Pyramid Lake, not to be confused with the other Pyramid Lake, a famous trout fishery in Nevada, is part of the extensive California Aqueduct system that brings water down from the San Francisco Delta. Created in 1974, this 1,300-surface-acre reservoir lies in chaparral-covered foothills north of Los Angeles at an altitude of 2,500 feet. The lake is warm enough for largemouth bass and panfish, but because of the constant flow of water into and out of the lake via the aqueduct and because Pyramid is steep, deep, and normally very clear, it also can support striped bass, trout, and smallmouth bass, all species that prefer colder water.

It was striped bass that first put Pyramid on the map for many anglers and ultimately removed trout from the picture. Introduced via the aqueduct (Oops!), stripers quickly adapted to Pyramid and grew rapidly on a fertile mix of threadfin shad and hatchery trout. A few years ago, the DFG decided to stop planting trout in Pyramid Lake, claiming that the striped bass were eating too many before local anglers could catch them. It's unlikely that was actually the case, and the department was attempting to cut trout allotments at the time, but whatever the reason, trout plants have ceased. Lake managers and local anglers have been trying to get trout plants resumed.

The suspension of trout plants has upset anglers who predicated their fishing tactics on imitation of the hatchery trout, using giant wood plugs painted to mimic a rainbow trout. Some fly anglers also adopted the "trout as a hatch" idea, timing their outings to trout plants and building their fly collections around designs imitating rainbows. Now that stocking has stopped at Pyramid, smaller flies that resemble threadfin shad, bluegills, crappies, and various minnows probably are more effective. Bear in mind, however, that striped bass are not always discriminating predators, and they do like a large meal, so don't quit using large flies entirely. Striper expert Alan Cole notes that threadfin shad in Pyramid can get quite large. Normally you would imitate shad of 2 to 3 inches in length at most, but he has seen some that grow to 5 or 6 inches.

If you aren't familiar with striped bass habits, it is wise to pay attention to what the lure and bait anglers are doing. From the summer and fall into the early winter, huge schools of threadfin shad roam the open areas of Pyramid. Bait anglers use a long-handled net to catch shad (cast nets are more effective, but are illegal in California), then they drift-fish the shad just below the schools so striped bass will see them. Fly anglers can adopt this tactic by drifting streamers on sinking lines to take stripers.

For this kind of fishing, a quality fish finder is a real asset. It isn't used to find the stripers themselves, although they often show up well, or to find bottom structure, as you would for largemouth bass. What you are looking for is the bait itself. Threadfin shad schools show as huge, cluttered signals on a sensitive finder, and by staying in contact with the shad, you usually will be within casting range of stripers. Sometimes you don't need fancy electronics: the tip-off is the frantic action of the shad as they try to avoid stripers, largemouth bass, and predatory birds like cormorants, grebes, and gulls. These surface melees can be seen from quite a distance, and carrying a pair of binoculars in the boat is not a bad idea.

While surface-busting schools of stripers can show anywhere at Pyramid, most striper anglers concentrate their trolling or drift fishing around Chumash Island at the south end of the lake and at the entrances of the bays on either side of Spanish Point. You also can find stripers right at the marina, and when the current is flowing into the lake through the power plant north of the marina, you may find concentrations of stripers there, as well.

Unfortunately, Pyramid, more than most lakes, is restricted in access points. There's almost no place other than the marina at the north end of the lake where you can reach the shoreline on foot, and Pyramid has steep, brushy sides that make wading or shore casting difficult. So this really is a lake for anglers with boats. While wading and float-tube fishing are permitted, you really need a boat with a motor to reach most of the likely spots where stripers will be found.

Services provided at Pyramid include a boat launch, boat rentals, bait and tackle, and food right at the lake. The U.S. Forest Service recently opened a 94-space campground just north of the lake. Other services can be found nearby in Gorman or Castaic. Pyramid is open 7 days a week. Day use fees are $6.00 per car, but there is no boat launch fee. Winter hours run from 7:00 A.M. to 5:00 P.M., and summer hours are 6:00 A.M. to 8:30 P.M. The lake is closed on Thanksgiving, Christmas, and New Year's Day. For information, call the marina at (661) 257-2892 or the main gate at (661) 257-2790. For camping information, call (661)248-6575.

SILVERWOOD LAKE

SPECIES: Striped bass, largemouth bass, bluegills, and crappies.
BEST TIME: Good year-round, but best from the fall though the late spring.
FLIES: Shad patterns such as white or chartreuse streamers with touch of silver or metallic blue in them. Silverwood also has large populations of hitch, a minnow with silvery sides and a dark back that grows as large as twelve inches that also was shipped south by the aqueduct from its

native waters near San Francisco, plus various other minnows and several kinds of perch. Fresh-water sculpins are also very common.

FLOAT TUBES: Yes. Wading also is permitted. There are plenty of access points, and there is some good, shallow structure to fish from a tube.

LOCATION: 30 miles north of San Bernardino near the top of Cajon Pass. Take Interstate 15 north to Highway 138, then turn east and go approximately 11 miles to lake entrance.

Some 80 miles east of Pyramid is Silverwood Lake. The last reservoir on the aqueduct before it disappears under the San Bernardino Mountains to reappear at Lake Perris, Silverwood has only 1,000 surface acres, but rates as a major striped bass fishery.

The lake has two arms, Miller Canyon and Cleghorn. Together, these form one side of a very sloppy H, with the more open part of the lake at the dam forming the other side and the channel running from the launch ramp and marina out to the dam forming the crossbar. The channel is where some of the best fishing is found.

(At the time of this writing, Silverwood was recovering from a lengthy drawdown that had occurred while a new water transportation outtake was being constructed. Concurrently, however, fish habitat at Silverwood was enhanced through the creation of large rock piles that used rubble from the construction activities. These, in turn, were surrounded with dozens of plastic "bushes" anchored to the bottom. A court action brought by the Southern California Bass Council also has required the Department of Water Resources to take further steps to restore the fishery at Silverwood. Measures being considered include introducing either spotted bass or smallmouths and enhancing the forage base for bass by stocking Florida-strain bluegills. Whatever action is taken, such measures can only help the fishery. Call the park office of the Silverwood Lake State Recreation area at the number listed below for an update on what has been done.)

Silverwood is stocked with rainbow trout during the cooler months of the year, and the marina area next to the launch ramp, where the fish are planted, has long been a regular hangout for striper fishermen.

Another hot spot for stripers is the water inlet from the aqueduct. When water is being pumped into the lake, stripers crowd in to take advantage of the flood of stunned and injured baitfish swept into the lake. Because of the swift current and the line of safety buoys to prevent boats from getting too close to the white water, however, this is not a good place for the fly fisher. It would take the double haul of a lifetime to get a fly to the right spot and a lead-core shooting head to keep the fly in the strike zone for more than a couple of seconds.

Instead, I would recommend that fly anglers work the many points in the main channel leading from the dam back to the marina. When water is moving through the system, Silverwood acts much more like a large, slow river than a lake, and methodically working moderate-sized streamers on full-sinking lines so that they approach the rocky points in the direction of the current should give you the best chance for success.

I can't emphasize enough the importance of these points along the main channel. The current sweeps bait and food from the dam and spillway south to the outtake towers near the launch ramp. The points and coves all have quick access to open water, and to deep water as well, something stripers favor. This makes for good fishing early and late in the day, and the trick is to fish the points on the east side while they are in shadow in the morning, then switch and fish the points on the west side as they draw into shade in late afternoon.

The two long arms, Miller and Cleghorn, are both visible from the launch ramp and marina. Both have road access (Miller Canyon has its own entrance), and you can park and walk along the bank, bicycle the paved bike path, or launch a float tube. Both have streams that flow from early spring on into the early summer and year around in very wet years. In the fall, the influx of fresh water attracts baitfish, particularly huge schools of threadfin shad, and some of the best fishing for stripers occurs when the leaves turn and there's enough flow in Miller and Cleghorn Creeks to bunch the bait up in the end of both arms.

Other key areas are the riprap along the face of the dam, the rock quarry area in the main lake, across from the dam, where steep walls often hold suspended striped bass and schools of shad, and the Live Oak area just to the east of the quarry. Live Oak is a boat-in picnic area, but for the angler, the main attraction is the large number of old, dead trees in the coves there. In particular, a large cove (called Quiet Cove on some maps) attracts many baitfish and lots of crappies and bass. Stripers prowl the edges, and the point that divides the Live Oak area from the quarry is another good spot to prospect with a sinking line. At Live Oak you can access the main lake via a dirt road (Forest Route 2N33) that winds around the eastern portion of the main lake. You can park along the road and walk down to the water on well-worn trails in several places.

On the west side of the main body of the lake there are a couple of turnouts on Highway 138 where you can park a car and walk down dirt roads to the lake in an area called Chemise Bay, which is another good striper spot. It's steep going, and doubly steep, it seems, coming out. You can walk the bank or wade in spots, but it's a much better float-tube spot.

At Silverwood, unlike Skinner or Pyramid Lakes, you can fish at night. Because of the many access points, trails, and the well-developed bike path, it's easy to get to the shoreline after the park is closed for the evening. The Silverwood Lake State Recreation Area is open from 7:00 A.M. to 7:00 P.M. from the end of September to around the first of April, and from 6:00 A.M. to 9:00 P.M. in the summer. After those hours, many anglers park their cars outside the state park and walk or ride a bicycle in to fish late at night, when the largest stripers may feed in water so shallow their back fins stick into the air.

Night fishing for stripers is doubly exciting. You hear big fish slamming bait, and every cast has the potential to produce a striper the size of a small cow. It's also a time when a big popper fished on a floating line may produce better than a streamer and sinking lines. I would suggest that during the day you scout the areas you want to fish, since you won't be seeing much at night. Make sure you wear a floatation vest in case you step into a hole. In addition, keep a sharp eye out for rattlesnakes, bears, and even the occasional mountain lion. You are restricted to shore fishing or wading after dark. Boats have to be off the lake by dark, and float tubing at night is illegal. It's been done, you understand, but it's illegal. One guy I know caught a 26-pound striper about 1:00 A.M. and it towed him around for nearly an hour before the exhausted fish finally gave up.

Silverwood is run by the state parks system and has a fully developed campground, including group camping facilities. There are two launch ramps, a full-service marina, and a number of picnic areas within the park. Two small stores are located nearby, and many services are available in the city of Hesperia, a few miles away. Day use fees are $6.00 per car, and the boat launch fee is $5.00. Camping fees are $17.00 per night, Sunday through Thursday, and $18.00 per night on Friday and Saturday from May 1 through October 31. Campsite reservations are made through Destinet, (800) 444-7275. There's day-use parking for more than 600 automobiles, and the park often fills on summer weekends. It can get hectic, but if you get there early it's usually OK. For more information, call the park office at (760) 389-2303 or 389-2281.

LAKE SKINNER

SPECIES: Striped Bass, crappies, bluegills, and largemouth bass. Hatchery rainbow trout in the winter.

BEST TIME: Good all year. From the fall into the early winter is good, but the spring is very good.

FLIES: Streamers that mimic threadfin shad. White and/or chartreuse patterns with dark backs seem best. All white with silver flash also is good.

FLOAT TUBES: No, and shore access is very limited. On the other hand. personal watercraft are not permitted, and that's a plus.

LOCATION: 90 miles southeast of Los Angeles Take Highway 60 through Riverside, then go south on Interstate 215 and Highway 215 to Temecula. Or take Highway 91 to Corona, then go south on Interstate 15 to Temecula. Turn east on Rancho California Road to reach the park entrance.

This 1,140-surface-acre reservoir operated by the Riverside County Parks Department is an oddity. It didn't get its striped bass from Northern California directly. Instead, they arrived from the Colorado River via an aqueduct and pipeline that covers a couple of hundred miles of desert and mountains. Small stripers must be unbelievably hardy to survive such a trip, but that's the nature of this gamefish.

Unlike all the other waters in the Southland with stripers present, Skinner offers a number of advantages to the fly fisher. Its relatively small size and shape concentrate the fish more than the other striper lakes in the area. Its location in lower Riverside County makes it accessible for anglers from both the San Diego area and the Los Angeles–Orange County complex. Add to that good facilities—a campground, store, dual launch ramps, and best of all, a 10-mile-per-hour speed limit with no jet skis, other personal watercraft, or water skiing allowed—and you have a first-rate fly-fishing lake. Unfortunately, there also is a ban on float tubes and wading. This makes Skinner a boat angler's lake, but not one that requires a large boat. Lake rules require a 10-foot minimum length, and you can fish a lot of it with just a good-sized electric trolling motor on a pram.

While you can't float-tube Skinner, the primary fly-fishing tactic is one with which any float tuber instantly will be comfortable. Early in the morning, and sometimes in the evening, you can find both shad and schools of feeding stripers in very shallow water in the east end of the lake. This shallow-water action occurs in the spring, when the shad begin to gather in huge schools in the warming waters of the back bays, and again in the fall, when surface waters cool enough for both bait and predators to rise out of deeper water.

When the shad go shallow, the stripers follow them in and rove like packs of wolves, busting into the shad and then moving on. Over the surface of the lake, action can be nearly constant, but it's never in the same place for long.

"It doesn't do a lot of good to pursue the schools—it just puts them down," said Bob Slamal. Bob operates Riverside Ski and Sport in Riverside. The "Ski" part is mostly snow skiing, and the "Sport" half is all fly fishing. As many days a week as possible, Slamal fishes and also guides for stripers and largemouth bass. His analysis of Skinner's stripers is worth noting. "We've found that getting in an area where you see indications of shad schools, then just waiting for the stripers to make contact is less likely to spook the fish."

Indeed, for more than an hour one clear winter morning, that proved to be the case. I fished with Bob and Luc Paquette, a friend of ours, using Bob's guide boat. Sometimes we would see frantic shad skipping across the water with boils of stripers right behind, but just out of casting range. Then, suddenly, they would be all around the boat, and we could get in a few casts, hook a fish or two, at which point the action would be over again for a few minutes.

After midmorning, the swirls of feeding stripers faded away, and we also noticed the bait anglers beginning to head for deeper water. Their game was to anchor or drift off the main lake points in 20 to 30 feet of water, intercepting small schools of stripers as they prowled around hunting for food. The action hadn't stopped, it just had moved.

We adopted a similar measure, again a tactic that float-tube anglers favor. By using a combination of a light breeze and a stout electric trolling motor, we drifted the boat across areas of deeper water, casting fast-sinking lines back along the direction of drift, then letting the fly sink until it was bumping the bottom. Things slowed in midday, but as the sun got lower in the sky, the action started back up, and we repeated much of the morning's action during twilight, with the exception that the shad and stripers did not repeat their back-bay behavior. Most of the later fish came from 15 to 20 feet of water.

This is typical of the action at Skinner. Except for the dullest time in the middle of the winter, late January and the month of February, and again in August and early September, you should find stripers. They are still there the rest of the time, and they don't quit eating, it's just that you have to search deeper water or time your outings to the trout plants in hopes that will stir a brief burst of action. The Department of Fish and Game has decided to cease stocking of trout at Skinner, but the county always has provided a number of stocked fish from private hatchery operations for anglers, and I don't expect that to stop. As the case of Silverwood shows, the DFG also can change its mind. Call one of the numbers listed below for an update.

Skinner is roughly rectangular, with a couple of arms to the east and a large dam across the west end. An extensive buoy line keeps you a distance from the dam and rules out the riprap as a place to cast for stripers. The inlet, where water swirls into the lake, is on the north side, not far from the dam, and there is a steep slope that runs for some distance east from there. The conventional-tackle striper anglers belly up to the buoy line at the inlet and bombard the white water right where the channel enters the lake with huge wood plugs thrown with surf-casting rigs.

As at Silverwood, this area attracts stripers to feed on the dazed and dying baitfish when the water is running. And as at Silverwood, it is not a great spot for the fly angler. You would need lead-core line and a two-handed salmon rod to reach anywhere near the swiftest current. However, the north shore all the way to the back of the northern arm is a place worth prospecting, either by locating ball of shad on a fish finder or by drifting and casting.

The south shore has lots of neat-looking coves and visible brush. The fishing there is not bad for largemouth bass, but I've yet to see many stripers in those coves. There are, however, a handful of humps associated with the points. These lie offshore in deeper water and seem to be magnets for baitfish. They should be checked often for the presence of a cloud of bait. The humps show up on the topo map made by Fish-n-Map, a good buy that includes Silverwood and Perris, as well as Skinner on one map. Anchoring and casting or drifting across these trailing a streamer can produce action, especially at times when stripers cannot be located in the shallow areas.

The marina and launch ramp #1 always hold some stripers, as does launch ramp #2 in the south arm. Both launch ramps can have groups of planted trout milling around them at the right time of the year, and if you happen to be there with a fly rod and a big streamer, it increases your chances of connecting with one of the lake's larger citizens.

Even most of the bait and lure anglers don't focus on the fact that striped bass are schooling predators and spend a lot of their time roaming open water. You may not be able to see obvious concentrations of fish, but if you drift right through the flat, bath-

Some lakes have hybrid striped bass. Known as "wipers," they are a cross between stripers and a smaller cousin, the white bass.

tub middle of the lake trolling flies on fast-sinking lines, you can get your arms jerked out of their sockets. This area looks like a desert, but in midday, the bait and the stripers sometimes retire to open water , so don't overlook this as an option.

The lake is open year around, and you can get information on entrance fees and camping by calling (909) 926-1541. There's a day use fee of $4.00 per vehicle, plus each angler needs a $5.00 fishing permit. State fishing licenses also are required. General fishing information can be had by calling the marina at (909) 926-1505. Anglers interested in guided outings can contact Bob Slamal at Riverside Ski and Sport, (909) 784-0205, or Frank Shelby at His and Hers Fly Shop, (714) 548- 9449.

CHAPTER SEVEN

SAN DIEGO COUNTY'S GREAT RESERVOIRS

LIKE ALL SOUTHERN CALIFORNIA CITIES, SAN DIEGO has been threatened with water shortages almost yearly, and from its beginning, practical plans for development have required a stable supply of water all year long. Starting in the 1800s, various entrepreneurs and agencies created a chain of reservoirs all around San Diego County. Water for business was their aim, but in bringing their projects to completion, they also created some exceptional angling opportunities for the fly fisher in what is perhaps the best set of warmwater lakes in the state, all located within one county and all within a couple of hours' drive of the center of San Diego.

This extensive system of water-storage reservoirs is now owned and operated by the City of San Diego. Impoundments with such names as El Capitan, Hodges, Miramar, Murray, Otay, Sutherland, and San Vicente are the stuff of legend for conventional-tackle anglers, having produced more largemouth bass over 10 pounds than almost any other place I know. These lakes, however, are less well known by Southern California fly-fishing enthusiasts, primarily because they offer more warmwater action than trout angling.

What transformed a reservoir system designed to provide water for development into an exciting fishery was the deliberate introduction of Florida-strain largemouth bass into these waters. Stocked in 1959 through the efforts of Dr. Orville Ball, a fishery biologist and lakes superintendent for the San Diego City Lakes, the Florida-strain largemouth turned a bunch of reservoirs with fair bass fishing into a select group of trophy bass factories.

Largemouth bass first were brought into California in 1874. Although the largemouths of the day were imported from all over, in general they were believed to be of one genetic type. And indeed, except for a difference in scale counts, which have to be undertaken by a qualified fishery taxonomist, there is no readily apparent difference between Florida-strain bass and their northern relatives. These days, however, it is generally accepted that largemouth bass from Florida and its surrounding states are distinct from those we now call northern-strain bass. The difference is simple: overall, Florida bass grow faster and larger than their northern cousins.

While most bass anglers, including myself, refer to "Northern-strain" or "Florida-strain" bass, in fact there are not many waters in Southern California that offer just one or the other. In most lakes, what you actually get is a hybrid of the two. These grow larger than pure northern fish and are marginally easier to catch than pure Florida bass. With the hybrids comes what biologists call "hybrid vigor." The hybrids grow faster and larger and are healthier and more disease resistant than either pure ancestor.

Jim Matthews admires a northern-strain largemouth bass taken near the dam at Barrett Lake. This relatively small impoundment is one of the better warmwater fisheries in San Diego County.

Sometimes it seems to me that I can sense the difference that the Florida-strain heritage makes in individual fish. There just is something about a bass from Florida-strain stock. Perhaps it is the chunky heft of the body. Even small fish have a blocky, substantial bulk that always seems to weigh more than is recorded on a scale. There's also something formidable in the emptiness of that round, black eye, as remote and alien as that of a great white shark. And make no mistake: in its freshwater environment, the largemouth bass is equivalent to the great white in its ocean home. Once it has grown too large to fall prey to another bass or be impaled by a heron or some other hunting creature, it absolutely dominates its surroundings. In short, there's more to these hybrid fish than just size. They have enough moods and layers of complexity in their behavior to be a continual puzzle, yet are aggressive and more than willing to take a fly.

Normally an ambush-style predator, largemouths have a reputation for lurking in the shade of a solid structure like a dock or submerged tree and waiting for some luckless creature to happen by. The range of foods they will eat includes whatever they can get their mouth around, and while they are introduced sport fish, bass reproduce in the waters they are stocked in and seldom require any restocking. The bass you catch in California are as wild as any stream-bred trout.

Their cavernous mouth and the surrounding tissues are mostly bone and bloodless membrane, which also makes them a fish almost designed by nature to be caught and released. Not only that, their lower jaw is a built-in handle allowing you to lift them out of the water and return them without handling the body of the fish. Bass weighing more than 6 or 8 pounds should be supported both by the jaw and the belly, however. Their jaw never was meant to hold that kind of weight.

Referred to by a number of outdoor writers as "America's Fish," the largemouth bass is, I believe, a vastly under-utilized sport fish for fly anglers. Largemouths will take a wide variety of flies, respond to both surface and subsurface presentations, and especially in Southern California waters, grow to awesome proportions. The California record for largemouth bass had been only some 14 pounds prior to the introduction of the Florida bass. The record (from Lake Castaic, in the Los Angeles area) now stands at over 22 pounds, and the record for the San Diego City Lakes is a "mere" 15-pound, 5-ounce bass from El Capitan.

I can cast flies to bass weighing no more than a pound or two all day and enjoy every minute of it, and I mention these records not to turn fly anglers into record hunters, but to point out the potential of these well-managed waters. It adds something to your fishing day when each and every cast might result in being suddenly attached to the largest fish you've ever caught on a fly.

Of course, waters in San Diego hold more than largemouth bass. For a near-desert in the extreme south of the state, San Diego County does have its fair share of trout fishing, though in

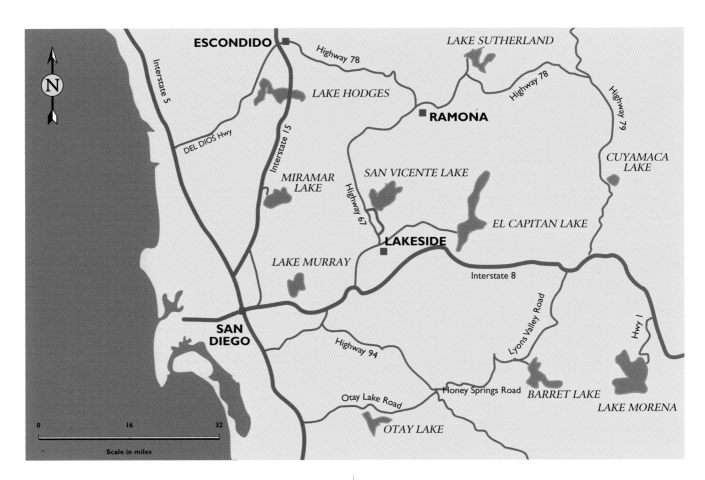

lakes it is of the put-and-take variety. Despite that, the chance to tangle with a hard-fighting rainbow of 2 or 3 pounds isn't bad, and often the trout can be much bigger. The area has good fishing from Lake Cuyamaca, nestled in a pine-tree-ringed meadow at 4,700 feet to Hodges at only 300 feet above sea level. Between waters operated by the City of San Diego, the county, and other agencies, you have nearly every type of stillwater fly fishing you can imagine.

One reason for the success of the sport-fishing program of the San Diego City Lakes chain is the management style, which has been adopted by the operators of many of the other lakes around San Diego County. None of the 9 lakes is open 7 days a week or all 12 months of the year, although they are open more often now than they used to be. Most are open 3 or 4 days a week, with enough overlap that you can always find one or more open on any given day. Yearly opening dates are dependent on winter rains and lake levels, but generally they open in March or April and close for maintenance in late October or November. Most are closed for only a few weeks, at most.

The City Lakes have a good information hot line at (619) 465-FISH (3474). There also is a web page at www.ci.san-diego.ca.us/water/recreation/index.html. Information numbers for lakes listed in this chapter other than the San Diego City Lakes are given at the end of the relevant entry. The other waters in the county have their own schedules, but most are open year-round. Those that stock trout do so in the winter months,

with the exception of Cuyamaca, whose altitude allows year-round trout fishing. In all the San Diego City Lakes, and most of the rest in the county, float tubes are permitted, provided you wear a floatation vest and enough international orange to keep you from getting run over by boats. A deer hunter's baseball cap will do the trick. As a bonus, at most San Diego City Lakes, float-tube anglers can buy an advance ticket that allows them onto the water half an hour before sunrise.

BARRETT LAKE

SPECIES: Northern-strain largemouth bass, panfish.

BEST TIME: April through June and September through October.

FLIES: Bass bugs, streamers, Woolly Buggers, and shad imitations.

FLOAT TUBES: Yes. Obey the regulations concerning floatation vests and visible clothing. Private boats are not allowed. Rental boats are available.

LOCATION: Southern San Diego County. Take Interstate 8 from San Diego to Japatul Road, then turn south and watch for Lyons Valley Road. Take Lyons Valley Road 1.7 miles to the locked gate at the entrance to Barrett Lake. Anglers are escorted by lake staff through private property from there to the lake. For information, call the City Lakes Office at (619) 668-2050.

The hottest bass fly-fishing lake in a county famed for Florida-strain bass contains primarily northern-strain bass. If that sounds strange after my raving about hybrids of Florida-strain largemouth, so be it. Barrett Lake is a phenomenon. Closed to public access for many years, it finally reopened in 1994 by The San Diego City Lake Program. It was an instant hit. Dazed anglers reported 50-to-100-fish days. It wasn't just the numbers that stunned people, either. A reasonable percentage of the bass in Barrett weigh 7 pounds or more, and it's possible to catch and release two dozen bass all weighing around 3 or 4 pounds in a morning. Northern-strain largemouth bass do not grow to the tremendous size of their Florida cousins, but they make up for it with a hell-for-leather approach to hitting a fly that leaves you dizzy when the action is hot.

"To me, Barrett is one of the most interesting fishing stories in the west," said Jim Brown. Brown is the recreation director for the City Lakes Program. A fly angler himself, Brown labored for years to solve access problems through the private ranch lands that surround Barrett. He is justly proud of the effort it took to get Barrett opened up for angling.

"People come in and are just falling all over themselves to tell you about the numbers of bass they caught on their day at Barrett," Brown said. "It's far less important how big the numbers are than the fact that the fishing is very, very good. What is happening is that many anglers go home feeling they had the fishing experience of a lifetime."

Limiting the number of anglers allowed on the lake each day is what makes this quality angling possible. The complicated lottery system that originally was used to select anglers has been replaced by a simple first-come, first-served ticket process. Controlled entry via ticket sales through Ticketmaster (phone (619) 220-8497) restricts the number of anglers to a maximum of 100 per day, a number that is not always reached. This system preserves a feeling of isolation for the anglers who get tickets. Each angler with a ticket can bring three guests, for a total of four people per boat.

At 811 surface acres, Barrett is of fair size by Southern California standards. It is a water-storage reservoir located in low, oak-covered hills near the Mexico border not far north of Tecate. There are homes and ranches in the immediate area, but so far, the shores of Barrett have escaped development. You can scan the horizon and—except for the dam keeper's residence—not see a single building on the skyline. Instead of condo sprawl, Burger King signs, and gas stations, you get herons, grebes, and the occasional eagle to keep you company.

Fishing Barrett has a dreamlike quality. It has the flavor of a Ray Bergman bass fishing story from the 1940s. There's a pastoral feeling that puts you in a rocking-chair mood as you cast flies over waters that offer perhaps the best bass fishing in the state. As good as the fishing is—and it can be phenomenal—the experience itself is what you remember weeks afterward.

The first thing you notice is the silence. I'd be willing to bet that many urban Californians have experienced this kind of quiet only on waters they had to wear a backpack to reach. Frogs sound like kettle drums in the reeds, and wavelets slapping the side of your float tube startle you. Dragonflies go whining by like helicopters.

You can clearly hear the slurping sounds of bass ripping into schools of frightened shad a hundred yards away. The occasional excited voice you hear is another angler in a float tube at twice that distance. He sounds like he's next to you as he talks to his fishing partner about a big bass that just snatched a bass bug and is towing him around in circles.

Part of the feeling of isolation comes from the way you enter the lake. You can't just drive in. You must be escorted in a convoy down several miles of dirt road. It's one of the measures to which the city was forced to agree in order to get permission from land owners around the lake to allow access. The city runs convoys in for several hours on the hour each fishing morning and then repeats the process several times each evening to allow anglers out again. It sounds cumbersome, but they do it very well.

The main forage base for the bass at Barrett are enormous schools of threadfin shad. During much of the season, anglers can find the bass schooled up in the morning and again in the evening pursuing the shad in open water. It's exciting. Sometimes the boils of feeding fish and the raindrop spatter of fleeing shad across the surface cover a circle fifty yards in diameter. Even more thrilling, the boil to which you are casting to is just one of several within eyesight. You can get flustered and not get a strike, trying to cast to too many places at once, but that doesn't happen often.

The bass are skittish when feeding on top. You can't run a rental boat right into the boil and expect the bass to stay around. Instead, try cutting the engine early and letting the boat drift slowly within casting range, or bring along an electric trolling motor. A portable depth finder would be a luxury, not a necessity.

Throwing big poppers or skipping bugs at swirls requires a fairly stout stick to toss a wind-resistant popper or hair bug any distance. I would recommend a 7-weight to 9-weight rod and a good bass-taper line for this. Later in the day, when you are prowling the shoreline or the many submerged trees in the Hauser arm of the lake, smaller bugs, streamers, and sinking flies are easily handled on a 6-weight or 7-weight rod. Think about taking a 4-weight or 5 weight along, as well. Barrett is famous for bass now, but it is also alive with fat, hand-sized bluegills that school around the weed beds and come to investigate every small thing that falls to the surface.

By midsummer, the shoreline that isn't rocky has large green weed beds just offshore. The outside edges drop away into deeper water. These hold bass and bluegills. Both rocky and weed-choked areas have many partly submerged trees and clumps of brush. There's just so much good cover for bass it's hard to decide just where to fish.

If you've already gotten the impression that northern-strain largemouth aren't too particular about what fly patterns you present them, you're right. Anything that resembles threadfin shad works. Cork or foam-bodied popping bugs in white, silver, or fish-scale patterns are excellent choices for the top-water action in the mornings and evenings. Streamers that look like shad also are excellent. Lefty's Deceivers in almost any size get enthusi-

astic responses. White as a base color is best, but chartreuse, for some unexplained reason, also is very good. I like my streamers to have a fair amount of Flashabou or other shiny material along the sides and prefer patterns with prominent eyes.

Other patterns that would be successful include Woolly Buggers, both light and dark, Whitlock Eelworms, and any crayfish patterns. Actually, small streamers of just about any kind will work, but especially those tied with dark backs, white bellies, and a bit of flashy material. Larry Dahlberg's diving minnow designs also should work well, and I always would include something that sinks quickly, such as a Clouser Minnow, for midday fishing.

Leader shy these fish ain't. That's one of the great things about bass angling. When a bass decides it wants your offering, it is going to get it. You could have it attached to a mooring cable and it wouldn't make any difference. I would recommend a leader as simple as a 3 or 4 feet of 12-pound test, cut down to a one-foot stub for sinking lines. If you want tapered leaders, by all means use them, but it isn't necessary from the bass's point of view.

The season at Barrett runs from late April through September. It used to be open three days a week: Wednesday, Saturday, and Sunday, but at the time of this writing has been open only on Saturday and Sunday. This might be reversed in the future if demand warrants. Call the city hot line, (619) 465-3474, for the latest information on Barrett and all other San Diego City Lakes. Each angler selected can bring 3 guests, for a total of 4 people in a boat.

The convoys that control entry from the highway gate to the launch ramp make the run at 5:00, 7:00, 8:00, and 9:00 A.M. In the evening, anglers are able to leave at noon, 2:00, 4:00, 6:00, and sunset.

You may bring and launch your own float tube, but you still really need a boat to get around the lake. You also may fish from the shore if you choose, but again, a boat is essential to get anywhere worth fishing, and there are no roads or trails around Barrett. Rental rowboats are available for $8.00 daily. A boat with motor costs $25.00, or you may supply your own motor up to 20 horsepower. Currently, the fishing fee per angler is $4.00 per adult over 16 and $2.00 for those aged 15 and under. A valid California fishing license is required, and anglers shouldn't forget the requirement to wear it. If you are an out-of-state angler, you need either a nonresident license for $74.80 or a two-day license for $10.00.

Barrett is intended as a catch-and-release-only bass fishery. Flies must have barbless hooks, which means you may have to alter a few of your favorite bass bugs to fish here. You probably won't notice much difference in your catch/loss ratio. Normal state limits apply for bluegills, sunfish, crappies, and bullhead catfish.

Float-tube anglers often search for rainbow trout in the main channel of Cuyamaca Lake. This body of water is located in the Cleveland National Forest, east of San Diego.

Because Barrett sits in the least-crowded section of southern San Diego County, there aren't many services close by. It's best to find lodging and food in El Cajon or San Diego itself and get up early to make the drive to the Barrett entrance gate. Another option is to stay at Lake Morena County Park or the nearby Lake Morena Village. It's a fair drive east of Barrett on Interstate 8, but has the advantage of allowing you to fish Morena, another excellent fly-fishing water. (See below.)

LAKE MORENA

SPECIES Largemouth bass, rainbow trout, crappies.
BEST TIME: Good all year. From February through April is best for bass. From November to February is best for trout.
FLIES: Streamers, leeches, and bass bugs for bass. For trout, try Woolly Buggers in dark colors and small dry flies
FLOAT TUBES: Yes. San Diego City Lakes regulations apply. Also private boats are permitted and rental boats are available. Much of the shoreline on north end of the lake also is wadeable.
LOCATION: About 60 miles southeast of San Diego. Go east on Interstate 8 to Buckman Springs Road, then south about 9 miles to the entrance of Lake Morena County Park.

Unlike the much better known chain of bass-producing reservoirs like Barrett that form the San Diego City Lakes system, Lake Morena lies in rugged country not far from the California-Mexico border. At an altitude of 3,000 feet in the Cleveland National Forest, it is low enough to be a quality warmwater fishery, yet it also is capable of sustaining a very good put-and-take trout fishery during the winter months. Morena is a water-storage reservoir of around 1,500 surface acres when full, and is the centerpiece of a regional park. At capacity, it has 20 miles of shoreline consisting of jumbled piles of boulders and brushy stands of dead trees, nearly an ideal habitat for both fish and fishing.

Morena is the only lake in the state to hold an International Game Fish Association line-class record for fly-rod-caught largemouth bass. The record is not a new one. Ned Sewell of the San Diego area set the mark in 1984. His 13-pound, 9-ounce largemouth set an 8-pound-tippet mark that still stands today.

Morena has no threadfin shad, the primary forage base for almost all other California lakes that hold largemouth bass. Threadfin do not survive well in Morena during the cold winters. Bluegills, crappies, and hatchery trout are the primary food for the bass. Morena has lots of steep and deep shoreline, especially at the dam end of the lake, but it also has even more rocky, boulder-filled coves and points stuffed with brush and old scrub. The entire northern end of the lake, which is dry pasture during dry years, is under water when the wet years return. Much of it then is wadeable shallows, and all of it is good for the tube angler.

Flies of choice for the bass include poppers or Woolly Buggers, Muddler Minnows, olive Matukas, and big stonefly nymphs. A Clouser Minnow in chartreuse and white fished on a floating line is a good choice for bass, and in small sizes can be great for crappies, too. The western shore seems to have the best crappie fishing, but they move around a lot. Anglers heading to Morena (or any of the bass lakes in Southern California) would do well to use larger flies fished on deep sinking lines at least part of the time. The traditional popper on a floating line is great, and will catch fish, but if you are interested in the big ones, getting a larger fly deep is the way to go.

As noted, the forage base at Morena consists mostly of bluegills and crappies. Both panfish grow to respectable size, so even saltwater-sized flies are not out of line as imitations. Deceivers, Bend Backs, or any large baitfish imitations will do the trick. Bottom dredgers such as Edgewater's Wiggle Craw and old standbys like Dave Whitlock's Eelworms and the Hare Water Pup are excellent patterns for searching out the larger bass. And, of course, it wouldn't hurt to include a few leech patterns. A leech pattern caught the record bass at Morena.

Remember also that trout are stocked during the cooler months and that an 8-inch streamer with the pinks and greens of a rainbow isn't out of line if you want to find yourself connected to a really big bass—and that, of course, is what Morena is capable of producing. Can it happen? Absolutely. Will it? Nobody knows, but it will be a heck of a lot of fun for the angler who is in the right place at the right time.

One thing is almost certain. Given the conditions, Lake Morena is more than capable of connecting fly fishers with bass in the 5-to-10-pound range. It may not be the nearly sure thing that the more strictly controlled Barrett Lake nearby has become, but Morena might well be one of California's best fly-fishing lakes.

In addition to the prospect of trophy-quality largemouths and good panfish angling, Morena supports a better than average put-and-take trout fishery in the cooler months of the year. The fish are purchased by the county. They come from the Whitewater Hatchery, which has a reputation for producing quality rainbows. In recent years, the park has taken to stocking all it's trout for the season in just a few weeks, creating a large "resident" group of trout. The fish acclimate to the lake well and provide very good trout angling right through the winter.

Members of the San Diego Fly Fishers who fish Morena and nearby Cuyamaca on Wednesdays note that some old standby flies work well. They recommend Woolly Buggers, size 16, on sink-tip lines as a good starting point. Black and olive are the most effective colors.

Hugh Marx, manager of Cuyamaca Lake and a dedicated fly angler, likes Morena early in the season when it's too cold at his lake. Because of Morena's lower altitude, the fly action picks up earlier in the year, and Marx takes advantage of Morena's trout while the fishing at his lake still is mostly dominated by the bait crowd. He said that during January, February, and March—even into April—Morena can be a great place for trout fishing.

"My favorite spot is on the north shore near the old Honor Camp," Marx said. "For the most part, it's a very long and shallow area, and a float tube isn't necessary. Waders are helpful while the water is still cold. Typically, we fish streamers for the trout. Olive Matukas, size 6, 8, and 10, and olive-black Woolly Buggers in the same sizes. Also a fly known as the Rainbow Trout Fly is very good."

Marx said he and friends usually fish in the afternoon, during the last two or three hours of daylight, and he surprised me by describing better than average dry-fly fishing on cool winter days. "The last half-hour of light, the dry-fly bite can be phenomenal. The best is a *Callibaetis* emerger or an Elk Hair caddis in size 14 to 16 for both flies. We do what we call 'bobber fishing.' We cast the fly toward working fish, but since you can't tell which direction they are going, it's a guess, so you just sit and try to keep the fly as motionless as possible until the fish sees it and hits it."

Tiny Morena Village has a tackle shop, but it carries no fly-fishing gear. For fly anglers, the places to check is Stroud Tackle, 1457 Morena Boulevard, San Diego, (619) 276-4822, or the San Diego Fly Shop, 4401 Twain Avenue, Suite 6, San Diego, (619) 283-3445.

The fishing fee for adults is $3.50 daily, $2.00 for seniors and disabled anglers. Boat rentals are $8.00 per day, $25.00 for a boat with a motor, and you may launch your own boat without charge. The speed limit on the lake is 10 miles per hour, and personal watercraft are not permitted. just sailboats and sailboards. If you plan on float-tube fishing, don't forget your required flotation vest and international-orange baseball cap

Morena is open all year around and has a large campground with over 100 sites, most with hookups. Fees for camps are $12.00 for primitive RV and tent camps and $16.00 for sites with hookups. If you have 10 vehicles or more in your party, you can make group camp arrangements by calling (619) 565-3600. Another neat deal is the availability of two rental cabins that will sleep a number of anglers for $25.00 per night.

For more information on fishing, camping, and other recreation, call (619) 694-3049. Camping reservations are not required, but if you want them, call (619) 565-3600. Morena has a 24-hour taped fishing report at (619) 478-5473. The county park's office number is (619) 579-4101.

CUYAMACA LAKE

SPECIES: Rainbow trout, smallmouth bass, and Florida-strain largemouth bass.

BEST TIME: The early spring through the late fall for all species.

FLIES: For trout, Woolly Buggers in black or olive are hard to beat. There is dry-fly action early and late in the day, but streamers or nymphs are more appropriate. For bass, small popping bugs, frog imitations, and large dry flies all work. The best bass action is at the south end of the lake in the summer, Weedless fly designs are needed. The primary forage fish for both bass and trout is the golden shiner, so make sure your streamers have a little gold or orange in them.

FLOAT TUBES: Yes. Obey San Diego City Lakes regulations. Rental boats also are available and private boats are permitted. Some of the south end is wadeable for bass and panfish.

LOCATION: Inside Cuyamaca State Park. Take Interstate 8 to Highway 79, then head north to park. It's about 50 miles from San Diego.

Anglers from the Los Angeles area might choose the scenic route, leaving Interstate 15 at Temecula and traveling east and south on Highway 79, through Julian.

At first it seems a bit like magic. You've scarcely left the metropolitan sprawl of San Diego and its surrounding cities behind when suddenly you're transported from the dry, chaparral-covered hills of Southern California to a High Sierra setting. Covering just 110 surface acres, Cuyamaca is not a large lake, even by Southern California standards. Maps of the lake would lead you to believe it's much larger, since most outline a normally dry meadow to the northeast that is separated from the regular lake by a dike. Only in very wet years does this area flood and become part of the lake.

What it may lack in size, Cuyamaca makes up in performance. It is a first-rate put-and-take trout lake operated by the Lake Cuyamaca Recreation and Park District. Hefty rainbow trout from the privately owned Whitewater Hatchery are stocked nearly year around, and this is augmented with substantial stocking of trout by the California Department of Fish and Game.

The current record for trout from Cuyamaca is a portly 14 pounds, 1 ounce set in October 1995. While trout like this aren't caught every week, it's common to find vibrantly colored rainbows of 2 to 3 pounds being taken, and 5-fish limits of plump 10-to-13-inch trout are not a surprise.

Before you turn up your nose at the idea of stocked trout, consider this: San Diego County is as far south as you can get in California and still be in the United States. Trout water and mountains are at a premium, and Cuyamaca represents a real resource to the fly fisher who wants to cast a fly over trout without driving several hundred miles to reach the Sierra or points north. Whitewater Hatchery rainbows are chunky, robust fish that look and act wild. They enter the lake already weighing over a pound (many are 2 or 3 pounds or more), and they grow quickly in Cuyamaca's rich cornucopia of aquatic insects and invertebrates. They are a handful on a fly rod and can give you a thrill not to be underestimated.

Cuyamaca's year-round trout season is unique in this part of Southern California. The lake's 4,700-foot altitude insures that waters remain cool enough for trout right through the summer, not just in the cooler months of winter, and while the winter months are cold, with occasional snowfall, they usually are clement enough to allow anglers to fish right through the year.

Because of the generally good trout fishing, and the float tubing, Cuyamaca is getting more attention from fly anglers in recent years. Midweek outings have become a tradition for a group of anglers from the San Diego Fly Fishers club. Calling themselves the "Wednesday Bunch," these anglers concentrate their efforts on trout.

"We have two flies which the trout really respond to at Cuyamaca," noted Ned Sewell, a member of the Wednesday Bunch. "One is an olive Woolly Bugger, and the second is a Woolly Bugger variation that has a black tail and body and a special red hackle for the palmer wrap and a good, wide band of gold ribbing." They see a lot of little damselfly nymphs at Cuyamaca, really tiny ones, about size 16, and that could account for the olive color working so well.

As you walk the shoreline, you'll also see huge numbers of little minnows in the shallows. Some of these are baby bass and bluegills, but there's also a huge number of golden shiners in the lake, making a solid forage base for all the larger trout and bass. Shades of olive with a hint of brass or gold wire would imitate these well. The imitations don't have to be all that small, either. Anglers fishing bait for trout have caught shiners up to 9 inches long, and with a number of trout in the 5-to-10-pound range roaming the lake on any given week, fishing a saltwater sized streamer might be a productive alternative. A sink-tip line is the most effective for trout. Cuyamaca isn't deep enough for a full-sinking, being only about 20 feet at the deepest. A sink-tip gets the fly down, and also allows it to ride above the weeds on the bottom.

Other patterns that would be appropriate include Matukas in olive or black, Woolly Worms, and small streamers that would mimic the tiny shiners and other fry. Several anglers also said a Hornberg is a good fly here.

"Dry flies really work well in the evenings," said Hugh Marx. An enthusiastic fly angler, Marx recommended a small, olive no-hackle pattern as a good starting point. "An Adams or other general-purpose dry is a good fly—I'd go with something like an Adams Irresistible or olive Humpy to get extra floatation."

The Wednesday Bunch also finds time to cast flies for the lake's big, hand-sized bluegills and its bass. The weedy, reed-choked shallows at the south end of the lake hold schools of respectable bluegills that are ideal for warm summer evenings and tiny cork poppers. The bluegill fishing can be downright heart-stopping when the fly goes under in a swirl and you find yourself connected to an angry bass. The current lake record for bass is 14 pounds, 1 ounce, and a really large, pissed-off specimen can snap a tippet designed for panfish like it was a wet noodle. The bass and bluegills are underused resources for fly fishers at Cuyamaca. Trout, of course, are what bring most of them there.

Anglers can fish Cuyamaca successfully from the shoreline—using waders is OK—and both rental boats and privately owned boats can be used on the lake. Cuyamaca allows float tubes on weekdays and for a short interval after the boats must leave the water on weekends—a good time to fish anyhow. Monday through Friday, anglers can launch their doughnut-shaped craft and fish anywhere they like. Tubing is not allowed during the busy period on weekends for safety reasons

In the evenings, when some fly anglers like to fish the south end for bluegills and bass, wading the shoreline is the preferred way to find fish. The shallow south arm of the lake is the best place to wade. It's tough fishing there from a motorboat, since the weeds tend to clog props, and tubing can be difficult, as well. The shallow flats are choked with weed beds and ringed with bulrushes.

"We wade the south end of the lake, where there's lots of weed beds, and float tube the middle and north end of the lake," Sewell said. "You can tube the south end, but it's tough getting through the weeds, and it seems to put the fish down. A floating line and small cork poppers, more like bluegill sizes than larger bass poppers, seem to be the trick."

The lake has had Florida-strain largemouth for several years, but a number of smallmouth bass were introduced in the mid-1990s, and the lake's manager's hope they will do well in this higher-altitude water. This is the only San Diego area water with smallmouths. Fishing for them is limited to catch-and-release only.

Because Cuyamaca it is located close to state park facilities, nonfishing family members can find other forms of recreation, from horseback riding to hiking and bird watching, while you are fishing. Cuyamaca is also a fine spot to see fair numbers of deer feeding early in the morning and again in the evening during the spring and summer. In addition to all this natural beauty, the trout are strong, well proportioned, and since it is a put-and-take fishery, it is not only permissible to take a couple for the table, it's a good idea.

Cuyamaca charges a $4.75 daily fishing fee for adults. Children between 8 to 15 are $2.50, and those younger than seven must be accompanied by a paying adult. Boat rentals are $12.00, motorboat rentals are $25.00, and the fee to launch a private boat is $5.00. They have half-day rates, as well. Camping is $12.00, and RV camping with hookups is $17.00. In addition to the 5-trout limit, lake limits are 5 bass, 25 bluegills, and 10 crappies. For more information, call the lake office at (760) 765-0515 or write to Lake Cuyamaca Recreation and Park District, 15027 Highway 79, Julian, CA 92026. There is also camping in Cuyamaca State Park, (760) 765-0755, which surrounds the lake, and lodging is available in the nearby community of Julian.

LAKE HODGES

SPECIES: Largemouth bass, crappies, and bluegills.
BEST TIME: The spring, from March through May.
FLIES: Larger streamers with lead eyes or weighted, also crayfish and waterdog patterns.
FLOAT TUBES: Yes. Private boats are allowed, and rental boats are available.
LOCATION: In the southern end of Escondido, just off Interstate 15. Take the Valley Parkway exit, then turn on Via Rancho Parkway. Take Lake Drive to the main gate.

Lake Hodges, located within the city limits of Escondido, some 30 miles north of San Diego, is an 1,100-surface-acre reservoir that, when full, winds along the old San Dieguito River channel from the dam back under Interstate 15. It's perhaps the most urban of the San Diego City Lakes, being surrounded by homes and businesses, and is only minutes from downtown Escondido. Despite that, the services at Hodges are pretty simple. There's a decent parking lot for boat trailers and tow vehicles, a good launch ramp, and a small snack bar and bait-and-tackle operation.

The lake generally opens in late February or early March. Fly anglers not used to the rush of bass enthusiasts for these events should be prepared to cope with long lines and lots of angling pressure. Opening day often finds a entrance road filled with boats and tow vehicles that have been there all night. This ruckus winds down in a few weeks, however, and things return to a more normal pace. Still, if you don't mind having to cast shoulder-to-shoulder with anglers in big bass boats, the first weeks of the season are the prime time to find large bass in shallow water—really large bass. The lake record is 20 pounds, 4 ounces.

Rated by several authorities as perhaps the California lake most likely to produce largemouth bass over 8 pounds, Hodges also has outstanding bluegill and crappie fishing. The dense stands of tules that grow along sections of the shoreline hold baitfish, tons of bluegills, and many of the bigger bass.

From the dam, the lake winds north toward Del Dios Bay, where the launch ramp and services are located, then turns east through the so-called Narrows and toward I-15. There's a clump of partly submerged trees in the bay that always is worth investigating for big crappies. In the dam arm, and along the Narrows, it's also worthwhile to investigate the tules and the steep, rocky areas along the shoreline.

Bernardo Bay and Felicita Cove are both areas where a lot of good-sized bass are caught, and this is also an area where there are many old trees standing in 8 to 10 feet of water. From Felicita Cove back under the I-15 bridge, you find classic largemouth bass habitat and perhaps your best opportunities for top-water fishing with bass bugs. Threadfin shad are the prime forage for the largemouth here, and you can get into periods of frantic action when schools of bass herd frightened shad to the surface and create violent, but short-lasting boils. It doesn't happen every day, but in the spring and fall, it's a good idea to watch all around you for the beginning of a boil.

You don't need anything more than a well-built cork or foam popper when casting to a boil. At such times, the bass aren't choosy. It's more a matter of getting the popper down in the right spot than of presenting the correct color or size. One trick that can up your success rate is to tie a small streamer on a dropper from the popper hook. Use a leader of 6-pound test or so anywhere from 12 to 30 inches long. I like to use a weighted streamer, usually white with a bit of tinsel flash, and if you aren't too fussy about what constitutes a "fly" for bass fishing, a one-sixteenth-ounce crappie jig also is an excellent choice. Often the bass with respond to the noisy surface disturbance of the popper, then blast the trailer instead.

Given the choice, I would spend more time fishing the tules than the rocks. I spent a day some years back electroshock sampling Hodges with Larry Bottroff, the city biologist. A specialist in big bass, Bottroff made a believer out of me by stuffing the probes well into the tule beds and finding some of the biggest bass we saw all day. The problem is finding ways to penetrate the tules to get at the fish.

Tules are tough. They seem to reach out and snag any fly you're foolish enough to throw into them. The stringy, fibrous stems and leaves are easy to hook, and it's almost impossible to free your fly. The stuff is like a saw, and thrashing around trying to dislodge the fly punishes the leader and spooks the fish. A good monofilament-loop weed guard is vital to fishing tules, on both sinking and floating flies. Try to target small openings and holes in the tule beds. Even with accurate casting, you can't always avoid a hang-up.

A stout leader also is a requirement. You are not as concerned with the size of the bass as you are with getting it out of the tule "jungle" if you get a strike. On other lakes, a leader testing around 4 to 6 pounds is OK, even for good-sized bass. On Hodges, I would not laugh at the angler who chose a 15-pound or even 20-pound-test leader. Keep them short, and don't bother to taper them. Also, I wouldn't risk my brand-new sixty-dollar super line here. An old, beat-up weight-forward, or even a level line from your junk box is better. You are after strong fish in a really nasty tangle of vegetation, and you don't have to cast much. If you are fishing in a tube, you can get pretty close and sort of flip the fly into an opening, then feed out a little line. Even just dipping the fly and leader into a hole can result in a awesome strike. Most often, however, you just see or feel a sharp twitch and the line begins to retreat into the brush. Set the hook hard, and hang on!

Ned Sewell, holder of an IGFA tippet class record for a 13-pound, 9-ounce largemouth bass from Lake Morena, hoists a nice-sized trout caught at Cuyamaca Lake.

Flies should be bulky and offer a substantial mouthful. It's possible to toss a floating fly into holes behind the tule edge in places, but this is really a place for sinking flies that nosedive quickly into the openings and head for the bottom. Rabbit-strip flies and flies with lots of soft, slinky marabou weighted with lead eyes or bead heads always are good.

Hodges has little to offer the wading angler, but there is some shoreline access in the area around the launch ramp and the parking area. For those in a boat or float tube, however, it is a fine lake. On the south side of the Barnardo Arm, next to I-15, there is a spot where you can park your car and walk in with your tube. As at most of the San Diego City Lakes, float-tube anglers who don't want to stand in line and miss the first hour or so of fishing can purchase an advance ticket that allows them to be on the water ahead of the boating crowd.

The fishing fee at Hodges, as at all of the San Diego City Lakes, is $5.00 for adults, with a $2.50 fee for youths from 8 to 15 years old. Children 7 and younger are free. Boat rentals are $12.00 per day, $8.00 per half day, and motorboats are $32.50 per day, $24.00 per half day. Limits are 5 bass, with a 15-inch minimum size, and 25 crappies. There is no limit on bluegills. Escondido is a good-sized town, and has all services, plus you can make a family trip out of a fishing expedition—the San Diego Wild Animal Park is just minutes away.

LAKE MURRAY

SPECIES: Rainbow trout and largemouth bass.
TIME: The best time for trout is from November to May. Bass fishing is best from March though September.
FLIES: Woolly Buggers, Clouser Minnows, and big, fuzzy nymphs work well. At times, midge dry flies are needed. For the bass, take along a few big streamers that imitate trout.
FLOAT TUBES: Yes. Private boats are allowed, and rental boats are available. There is a one-lane launch ramp.
LOCATION: East of downtown San Diego off Interstate 8. Take the Lake Murray Boulevard exit, turn north to Kiowa Drive, then turn left to the entrance.

A popular place for San Diego area fly anglers, Lake Murray is not only a trout lake, but perhaps one of the best lakes in the county for taking bass on a fly rod. The lake is full of feisty large-mouths. They will gang up on schools of bait, and you get brief periods of intense action. Conway Bowman, the lake manager and an experienced fly fisherman, says that at times, the bass action can be better than at Barrett.

Trout fishing is excellent too, even if it is put-and-take. Both the city and the state provide fish. The Whitewater Hatchery trout bought by the city often are the larger fish, with the state providing the larger numbers of fish. This is a recent change. For many years, the state did not stock here.

Woolly Buggers in olive or black are the standard. Clouser Minnows in small sizes are deadly for the trout as well as for the bass. In the spring, there often is a good midge hatch, but it usually requires a boat or float tube to reach the areas where the trout are feeding on midges. Otherwise, a sink-tip line with a streamer or attractor pattern usually works best.

The trout cruise around a lot, and the water in Murray is very clear. The backs of the coves are very good for wading early and late, but once the sun has been on the water for awhile, the trout move deeper. The trout will chase bait in the coves, so minnow patterns are best there.

While the trout are chasing the bait, they in turn often are being stalked by much larger bass. Anglers tell of seeing bass in the 10-pound range feeding on the trout as the trout chase the smaller fish. A large streamer that resembles a rainbow trout would be a good thing to have in your kit.

Murray is also a good lake for bluegills. July through September often is the best time. The trick is that these big Florida-strain panfish stay in deeper water than other bluegills. It's not often you find them shallower than 10 feet, and they're often closer to 20 feet down. Try using a full-sinking line and a small Woolly Bugger or nymph to reach them.

At 200 surface acres, Murray isn't large, but its close proximity to San Diego makes it a popular destination for anglers of all types, and it also has better access around the lake than some other local waters. It is one of three City Lakes that offer trout angling. The other two are San Vicente and Miramar, both covered later in this chapter. Lake Murray is open from November through September on Wednesdays, Saturdays, and Sundays. Trout are planted from November through May. The actual planting dates fluctuate slightly depending on water temperatures.

Fees are $5.00 daily for adult anglers, $2.50 for youths between the ages of 8 and 15, and children 7 years old and younger are free. Boat launching is $5.00, and boat rentals are $12.00 per day, $8.00 per half day, $32.50 per day for motor boats, $24.00 per half day, . No private motors are allowed on rental boats. Lake Murray also has hourly rentals of motorboats at $12.00 per hour.

EL CAPITAN

SPECIES: Largemouth bass, bluegills, and crappies.
BEST TIME: March through October.
FLIES: Poppers, hair bugs, and sinking patterns for bass.
FLOAT TUBES: Yes, but good access requires a boat. Rental boats are available, and private boats are permitted.
LOCATION: Northeast of San Diego. Go east on Interstate 8 to Lake Jennings Park Road, then east on El Monte Park Road to the entrance.

El Capitan is a lake that should be on the list of every fly fisher who likes tossing a surface popper for bass. A long, skinny reservoir of some 1,600 surface acres at capacity (which it seldom is—1,100 surface acres is probably a more accurate size), El Capitan is possibly the most scenic of the San Diego City Lakes. It has largemouth bass, bluegills, crappies, and redear sunfish. The limiting factor for the fly angler is that there is little shore access. Except for the main parking area and the launch facilities, there are no roads around the lake.

You can catch some nice fish in the Chocolate arm, where the launch ramp and facilities are located, but to reach the best fishing, which usually is in the upper half of the lake, you need a boat. For those anglers who prefer float tubes to boats, perhaps the best bet is to pool resources, with several anglers chipping in for a rental boat to use as a water taxi to get people and their tubes to the top end.

When water levels are high, the upper end, with its brush and dead trees, is a bass-bugging delight. There's lots of brush and rocky structure in both the main arm, where the San Diego River comes in, and in the smaller Conejos arm. Much of the shore is steep and rocky, with dense brush reaching right down to the waterline when the lake is full. Because there's lots of shoreline cover to hold bass in shallow water, El Capitan is a great place for fishing top-water patterns such as cork poppers, hair bugs, and large, bushy dry flies. In the spring, El Capitan's water often is slightly murky, or "stained," as bass pros call it, "and this limited visibility makes the bass susceptible to a floating fly, especially one that makes noise.

The clearest water often is found in the arm of the lake behind the dam. This area, unfortunately, is also home to personal watercraft. The rest of the lake is absolutely chock full of good bass-holding structure, steep walls peppered with huge boulders and rocky points and coves. There are a lot of trees in the main arm that give cover to baitfish and bass.

Hybrid Florida-strain and northern-strain bass are the dominant species. El Cap is not known for producing giant bass, although the record is a very respectable 15 pounds, 5 ounces. It is, however, one of those lakes that usually can be relied on to produce numbers of fish in the range of 2 to 5 pounds—the result of a 15-inch minimum size requirement, which allows largemouth to reach spawning size before being caught and kept. A typical El Cap bass weighs around a pound and a half and is robust, almost football-shaped.

Jim Brown favors El Capitan as a bass-bug lake, rather than one that needs deep-sinking lines and weighted flies, as some of the other San Diego City Lakes often do. Many of us who have fished bass bugs on Southern California waters started with a cork popper called Bass Poison built by the late Hank Neverka, a engineer from Brea, and Brown thinks the pattern still is an effective fly.

Hank Neverka championed float-tube fishing for bass for many years, and when I first saw Hank demonstrate his green canvas Fish-N-Float tubes in the 1970s, I bought both his ideas and a dozen of his hand-made "popping bugs." The canvas tube is long gone, but I still have a few Bass Poison poppers, now retired, and I model my own after Hank's design. Cliff Hamilton, a fly tier from Orange County, is keeping the Bass Poison popper alive with an uncanny copy. You can contact him at (714) 529-1094 if you are interested in fishing this classic cork bug.

Brown thinks a cup-faced popping bug cast tight to shore cover before the sun gets on the water is the ideal way to fish El Capitan. "I've used the cork poppers, deer-hair bugs, and a floating Marabou Muddler with success," Brown said. "I never have put much time into sinking lines. That kind of fly fishing for bass just doesn't interest me. I will sometimes fish sinking flies on a floating line and a long leader, getting the fly down 2 or 3 feet, and that's usually all you need at El Cap."

Most of El Capitan's length runs from north to south, and it is in a steep, rugged canyon. Early in the morning, fish the western edges until the sun peeps over the hills, then retreat to the eastern side. This still is in shade long after sunrise, and you can fish shadowed cover there until late morning. Then you can repeat the procedure in the late afternoon, again fishing the shaded western side until the sun sinks low enough to put the eastern side in shadow.

The fishing for other species at El Capitan is in many ways as interesting as the bass fishing. The lake does not have trout, but it does feature Florida-strain bluegills, redear sunfish, and one of the area's best crappie fisheries. Except for a brief few weeks of spring spawning activity, all three of these panfish species retire to deeper water most of the time. Early in the morning and again in the last half-hour of dusk, you may find them taking insects off the surface and chasing smaller fish in the shallows, but a weighted nymph on a sink-tip line often produces the best results. For the largest specimens of bluegills and redears, a fast-sinking line with the ability to get a nymph down 20 to 25 feet probably is best.

For crappies, whose diet consists primarily of small minnows, streamers or Woolly Buggers are the best bet. White with a bit of blue or purple Krystal Flash works very well for me. At times, these fish will swarm on anything colored yellow. However, for the most part, a more natural color scheme seems best. Smaller versions of the Clouser Minnow, size 8 or so, are ideal for crappies. Even the larger ones, which can run to a couple of pounds, don't put up a hard struggle, but since you usually find them in brush or the tops of drowned trees, you still need a tippet testing from 2 to 4 pounds.

One of the great things about crappies and bluegills or redear sunfish is the angler can take home a stout stringer full of these great-tasting fish without feeling in the least bit guilty. Prolific and hardy, panfish often overpopulate lakes and become stunted. Reducing their numbers can improve fishing, and as table fare, they are superior to most other fishes.

The area immediately around El Capitan has little in the way of services, but since you are only about 30 miles from downtown San Diego, and even closer to the communities of El Cajon and Lakeside, that isn't a problem. Lodging and all services can be found relatively nearby. For information on lake conditions and services, call the City Lakes hot line at (619) 465-3474. As at other San Diego City Lakes, fees are $5.00 daily for adult anglers, youths from eight to fifteen are $2.50, and children seven and under are free. Boat launching is $5.00, and boat rentals are $32.50 per day for motor boats, $24.00 per half day. Rowboat rentals are $12.00 per day, $8.00 per half day.

UPPER AND LOWER OTAY LAKES

SPECIES: Florida-strain largemouth bass, crappies, and bluegills.
BEST TIME: Late winter and spring. The last couple of weeks in October also can be good. Not a major summer lake.
FLIES: Bulky sinking patterns, crayfish imitations, and shad streamers.
FLOAT TUBES: Yes. Private boats are permitted and rental boats are available on Lower Otay. Upper Otay is restricted to float-tube or shore fishing only .
LOCATION: 20 miles southeast of San Diego, east of Chula Vista. Take Telegraph Canyon Road east from Highway 805.

Perhaps the best-known of the San Diego City Lakes, Lower Otay is a 1,266-surface-acre reservoir located only a few miles from the border with Mexico. It used to sit in isolation amid rolling, scrub-covered hills, but the building boom in lower San Diego County now has surrounded much of it. The upper end of the lake near the road forms the Otay arm, which always is interesting to fish in the spring, but for my money, the Harvey arm of the lake stretching to the east is the best bet for fly fishers. There's more standing timber and lots of shoreline tule growth to hold fish.

Otay is a bit different from most of the other City Lakes in

Ed Velton battles a large Whitewater hatchery trout at Cuyamaca Lake.

that you can get access to a fair amount of the shore. The trouble is, much of the shore also is covered with dense tules. Still, bank walking and float tubing are viable options, which is a good thing, because early in the year, Otay can get jammed with bass anglers and their boats. On weekends, you may have to get in line the night before to be sure of getting on the lake early or at all. The lake has just so much parking for boat trailers and tow vehicles, plus, there is a safety limit on how many boats can be on a lake of a certain size. The author knows this because in 1980, he and his equally fish-crazy bride spent their wedding night camped in the boat line here. Apparently it was a good idea. We are still married, and she still catches more fish than I do.

When water levels are high and the tules are flooded, fishing a bug just on the edge of the cover in the first hours of daylight and the last half-hour of evening sometimes is productive. For anglers with big bass on their minds, the eastern shore of the Otay arm is often a good bet, as are the rock piles at the mouth of the Harvey arm. While there will be times when the bass gang up on shad and explosive surface feeding occurs, often all that activity doesn't translate into a good bass-bug bite.

Florida bass and Florida-northern hybrids seem to respond better to a stealthy, sinking-line approach. Crayfish and threadfin shad are the prime forage here, and while crawling a fly with some heft to it along the bottom or through the branches of drowned trees may not be as exciting as expectantly tossing a bass bug, when something unseen grabs the fly and heads for the far horizon, it leads to a definite rush.

In addition to the bass fishing, Lower Otay boasts a sizeable population of Florida-strain bluegills. The lake record is 3 pounds, 8 ounces. Crappie fishing is also very good, with a record of 3 pounds, 6 ounces. You also might find yourself hooked to a blue catfish. These big, predatory catfish are known to take lures and the occasional fly, as well as bait. Since the lake record is an astounding 82 pounds (the fish was caught, weighed, and released) you could hook a rod-breaking behemoth by accident.

Both lakes are open Wednesdays, Saturdays, and Sundays from January to October, and although fishing at Lower Otay can be laid-back, during most of the early spring, you'll face lots of other anglers wielding conventional tackle, and on weekends, you can find two or three boats at every good spot on the lake. Wednesdays are better, but Lower Otay should be regarded not so much for providing a "wilderness experience," but for providing quality fish. Unlike El Capitan and Hodges, Lower Otay has a 12 -inch minimum size limit on bass.

Upper Otay is something very different. Only 80 surface acres, it was long used as a brood-stock lake for Florida-strain bass. It is located just north of Lower Otay, and you use the same entrance and parking areas. It was closed to all angling until 1996, and during its opening weeks, Upper Otay didn't show a lot of the big fish that most people thought were in the lake. Bass anglers are a close-mouthed bunch, however, and I suspect there are fair numbers of good-sized bass there. Many of the larger fish probably were poached during the years it was closed—a popular hobby for a few unscrupulous people. Jim Brown once told me the reason he wanted it opened to the public was he couldn't see any reason why the poachers should have all the fun.

Only float tubes and shore fishing are allowed, and that is Upper Otay's charm. It provides a place where you can launch a tube and not have to watch over your shoulder for multitudes of bass boats. It hasn't developed much of a track record as yet, but the lake has potential as a quiet place to fish in an increasingly urbanized area. For that alone, Upper Otay has merit. Like Barrett, this San Diego city lake is operated as a catch-and-release-only fishery for bass, with the same artificials-only, barbless hook regulations.

As at other San Diego City Lakes, fees are $5.00 daily for adult anglers, youths from 8 to 15 are $2.50, and children 7 and under are free. Boat launching is $5.00, at Lower Otay only, and boat rentals are $32.50 per day for motor boats, $24.00 per half day. Rowboat rentals are $12.00 per day, $8.00 per half day. The adult fishing fee is $5.00.

SAN VICENTE LAKE

SPECIES: Trout, bluegills, largemouth bass, and crappies.
BEST TIME: November through May for trout. In the summer, bass and bluegill fishing is restricted to Thursdays and Fridays only.
FLIES: Nymphs and streamers for both trout and bluegills. Smaller bass bugs and sinking patterns for bass.
FLOAT TUBES: Yes. Private boats also are permitted and rental boats are available.
LOCATION: Northeast of San Diego. Take Interstate 8 east to Highway 67 through Lakeside to Moreno Road, the follow the signs to lake.

San Vicente Lake, another reservoir in the San Diego City Lakes system, is nestled in steep, rocky canyon terrain 25 miles from San Diego. It is not a giant lake, around 1,000 acres when at capacity. It has lots of winding, rocky shoreline and a large island, Lowell Island, in the middle. In the past few years it has developed substantial grass beds, mostly milfoil and some pondweed.

San Vicente has a good-sized population of largemouth bass and crappies, and it is another of the City Lakes that stocks trout during the winter months, but the bluegill fishing may be the best in the area. It's always been considered a good lake for catching panfish, but in recent years, the bluegill population has simply exploded, and the catch rate has gone through the ceiling. Over the last few years, each week's reports from the lake indicate anglers catching thousands of bluegills—as many as 4,000 in one two-day fishing period.

"San Vicente will probably produce over 60,000 bluegills for anglers during the season from May to May," said City Lakes biologist Larry Bottroff. "It produced 45,000 bluegills in 1993, and 60,000 in 1994. One thing we have seen is that we don't have lots of very large bluegills, since many of these are younger fish, but we have numbers."

Still, there are lots of larger bluegills. Bottroff said he had heard of a 3-pound bluegill from San Vicente and had personally verified bluegills weighing 2 pounds, 12 ounces. There have been quite a few over 2 pounds caught. (The California record bluegill is a 3-pound, 8-ounce fish taken at Lower Otay in 1991.)

Despite such numbers, most anglers who spend a day at San Vicente key on the bass or trout and pretty much keep the bluegills on the back burner. That doesn't apply to a few bluegill enthusiasts who persist in trying to take the largest bluegill in the lake on conventional tackle. What they've learned about the behavior of these "new" bluegills will benefit fly anglers looking to connect with dinner-plate-sized panfish on light tackle.

"My biggest bluegill from San Vicente weighed 2 pounds, 9ounces," said Bob Ulery. A fanatic bluegill angler, Ulery lives nearby in Lakeside and fishes San Vicente regularly for bluegills and crappies. "One of the not-so-secret secrets of catching big bluegills at San Vicente is that in the spring, the largest bull bluegills will be out in deeper water, unlike the smaller ones."

San Vicente's steep shorelines seem to concentrate the larger males around submerged rock piles, old trees, or deep weed beds in as much as 30 feet of water. In addition to hanging out near rock piles, big bluegills also will choose the outside edge of the deepest weed beds in an area close to shallow spawning and feeding zones. Most of a bluegill's diet is composed of aquatic insects and tiny crustaceans, but they also feed on terrestrial insects that get blown into the water, and the largest bluegills will hunt and eat smaller fish, just like bass or crappies.

For those reasons, I would suggest that fly anglers abandon their floating lines and cork poppers and instead fish sinking lines with larger nymph or attractor patterns. A hand-sized bluegill may key on size 10 or 12 nymphs, but a dragonfly nymph tied on a size 6 or 8 hook may work better. Small streamers in the 2-inch range also will produce. And a 2-pound bluegill may hold at depths that require a full-sinking line, rather than a sink-tip.

Recommended locations for largemouth bass include around Lowell Island and the Barona arm of the lake. There's an old chimney that helps anglers locate excellent structure. Grassy Bay and North Bay are also noted as good starting points. San Vicente, like most clear lakes in Southern California, is noted by bass anglers as one that responds well to finesse techniques with light lines and delicate presentations on conventional tackle. Fly anglers would do well to emulate the approach. Smaller flies and lighter leaders will produce more bass here than on some San Diego lakes.

San Vicente is a good year-round lake, even though it's open to fishing for only a couple of days each week from Memorial

Day to Labor Day. The spring and fall are excellent periods, and San Vicente is one of the San Diego area's better winter put-and-take trout fisheries. That also helps make it one of the better lakes in Southern California for Florida-strain largemouth, since big bass become predators of trout and trout-sized baitfish. San Vicente is a great place to fish a big saltwater-style streamer designed to imitate a freshly planted trout.

As far as trout fishing itself goes, the winter should provide some good fishing, but instead of trying to find a major hatch and fishing dries, fly fishers would do better concentrating on wet flies and nymphs. San Vicente is a deep lake, and at only 650 feet elevation is often warm enough in the winter to send trout deep. In addition, the city has adopted a system of stocking all the trout for the winter season in a few short weeks in the late fall. The trout move into the deeper water, feeding on threadfin shad, and most of them are caught by trolling.

Like all San Diego City Lakes, San Vicente is open only on selected days. In the winter, it is open for fishing from Thursday through Sunday. In the summer, from Memorial Day through October, fishing is allowed only on Thursdays and Fridays, with the weekend reserved for water skiing.

Boats are rented only on fishing days, $12.00 for a rowboat for a full day, $8.00 for a half day, $32.50 per full day for a boat and motor and $24.00 for half a day. You may also rent a boat and use your own motor if it is under 25 horsepower. You may launch your own boat for $5.00. The day use fee per person the in winter when trout are stocked is $5.00 for adults and $2.50 for youths from 8 to 15, while children 7 and under are free. For more information, call the San Diego fishing hot line at (619) 465-3474.

MIRAMAR LAKE

SPECIES: Trout, largemouth bass, and panfish.
BEST TIME: For trout, November though May. For bass, from February to April.
FLIES: Matukas, Woolly Buggers, and nymphs.
FLOAT TUBES: Yes. Private boats are allowed, and rental boats are available.
LOCATION: 18 miles north of San Diego. From Interstate 15, take Mira Mesa Boulevard east to Scripps Ranch Boulevard and go south to Scripps Lake Boulevard, then east to the lake.

At just 162 surface acres, Miramar is the smallest of the San Diego City Lakes except for Upper Otay. It is a suburban impoundment, heavily stocked with rainbow trout during the winter months, but it also has both Florida-strain bass and bluegills. Despite the small size, it is reputed to hold some monster largemouth bass, and the lake record is twenty pounds, fifteen ounces, the largest bass ever caught in a San Diego city lake.

Miramar doesn't have a lot of open shore, although there is a jogging path around the entire lake. Much of the lake is surrounded with thick tules. This thick cover frequently is the target of float-tube fly rodders seeking bass. The trout tend to stay in the more open water and are sought by a growing number of fly anglers during the winter months. The weather usually is mild during the winter, and you can get in quite a bit of fishing. Water skiing and personal watercraft are not allowed, and the speed limit for boats on this small lake is 5 miles per hour, a definite plus for fly fishing.

One of the more developed City Lakes, Miramar has a quartet of fishing docks, a good launch ramp, and picnic areas. Trout anglers should try along the south side of the lake and the east side of Carroll Cove. A area on the south side known as Moe's Hole is reputed to be one of the best deep areas for trout. Bass and panfish normally are found near the shore reeds, but anglers casting big trout-colored streamers around the time of trout plants could connect with a trophy bass at the launch ramp. The largest bass key on the trout for food.

The lake is open to fishing all year on Saturdays, Sundays, Mondays, and Tuesdays, except for short maintenance closures, which typically happen in late October. As at the other San Diego City lakes, fees are $5.00 daily for adult anglers, youths from 8 to 15 are $2.50, and children 7 and under are free. Boat launching is $5.00, and boat rentals are $32.50 per day for motor boats, $24.00 per half day. Rowboat rentals are $12.00 per day, $8.00 per half day. Miramar also has hourly motorboat rentals for $12.00 per hour.

SUTHERLAND LAKE

SPECIES: Largemouth bass, bluegills, crappies, and redear sunfish.
BEST TIME: Good all season. May and June are very good, and September and October bring a repeat of the good fishing of the late spring.
FLIES: Small silver or white poppers, Woolly buggers, and small streamers.
FLOAT TUBES: Yes. Private boat are allowed, and rental boats are available.
LOCATION: 45 miles northeast of San Diego. Take Highway 67 from Lakeside or Highway 78 from Escondido.

If any of the city bass lakes could be considered a "sleeper," it is Sutherland. One of the smaller water-storage reservoirs that supply both water and quality angling to San Diego, it is also the most distant. About 45 miles northeast of the city, near the town of Ramona, it is a vaguely V-shaped 557-surface-acre lake at capacity, which it seldom is. Its 2,000-foot altitude makes it a little cooler in late spring and summer, and it is known for top-water bass action. This slight altitude difference also means that the spawn and the spring fishing start about the time they starts to taper off on Otay, Hodges, and the other lower-elevation lakes.

It's hard to think of a lake less than 50 miles from a major metropolitan center as "remote," but because of the number of quality fishing lakes that San Diego residents enjoy closer to home, Sutherland just doesn't get as much angling pressure. That alone should endear it to fly anglers, although it has not been much frequented by them. They are missing some excellent warmwater sport.

Access for float-tube anglers is fair. It entails some walking from the parking area to reach the better spots in the Santa

Ysabel arm of the lake, but there are no steep slopes to be negotiated in waders while carrying a tube. Conway Bowman, the reservoir keeper at Lake Murray, says Sutherland has one of the better bluegill fisheries in the San Diego City Lakes chain, and it is a first-rate bass lake as well.

Sutherland is famous for violent surface action. At times, it seems like the whole lake is churned to a froth by schools of bass busting threadfin shad on the surface. When this occurs, small white streamers or bucktails can work well, and poppers fished with a floating line stand a chance of producing fantastic results. Again, white or silver is a good match for the threadfin shad, and I like poppers with a bit of glitter or prism tape to add flash. Instead of feathers for the tail dressing, try some Mylar or Flashabou to add sparkle to the mix.

You might also try an old striped bass trick. Tie a 12 inches or so of 4-to-6-pound-test monofilament to the popper's hook and add a small fly as a trailer. This rig isn't hard to cast, and the fly sinks below the popper as you pause between strips. Bass charging into the fray mistake the sinking fly for an injured shad.

Like most of the San Diego area lakes, Sutherland has lots of brush and stickups for bass and panfish cover. The Santa Ysabel arm probably has more than the rest of the lake, and it also has a lot of broken-up rock and plenty of submerged trees. The more open Mesa Grande arm of the lake has less brush, but lots of rocks and boulders to hold fish. In addition, Sutherland and it's surroundings are quite beautiful. If Sutherland has a problem, it is that frequent drawdowns occur even in the best years, and in the past, Sutherland has gotten very low at times. This is a lake I would not fish without getting an update on water conditions from the city fishing hot line, (619) 465-3474, or Bob's Bait and Tackle in Escondido, (760) 741-1570.

The lake is open from April to October on Fridays, Saturdays, and Sundays. Fees are $5.00 for adult anglers, youths from 8 to 15 are $2.50, and children 7 and under are free. The lake has launch ramps that may or may not be usable depending on water levels. The boat-launch fee is $5.00. There are a pair of fishing piers, and the concession has rental boats and food and drink. Boat rentals are $12.00 per day, $8.00 per half day, and boats with a motor are $32.50 per day, $24.00 per half day. A motel and other services can be found in Ramona, 8 miles away. Also, there is a county park campground a few miles west of Ramona.

OTHER SAN DIEGO AREA LAKES

This is by no means a complete round-up of stillwater fly-fishing opportunities in San Diego County. There are a number of smaller county and city park lakes that offer recreational angling. Lake Wohlford and Dixon Lake in Escodido stock trout in the winter and have sizeable bass and panfish populations as well. (See Chapter 9.) Neither allow wading or float-tube fishing. Lake Henshaw, near Mount Palomar, is well known as a fantastic crappie fishery and has produced some huge bass, but it also forbids waders and float tubes.

San Diego has two fly shops that can provide information on the lakes covered in this chapter: Stroud Tackle, 1457 Morena Boulevard, San Diego, (619) 276-4822, and the San Diego Fly Shop, 4401 Twain Avenue, Suite 6, San Diego, (619) 283-3445. You might also contact the San Diego Fly Fishers at (619) 466-7569.

CHAPTER EIGHT

THE LOWER COLORADO

TO WRITE A COMPREHENSIVE FISHING GUIDE TO the entire Colorado River from its genesis in the high country of the Rocky Mountains to where it runs across the border into Mexico near Yuma, Arizona would be tough to do in two or three books. The Colorado is 1,400 miles of fishing diversity. Fortunately, we're concerned here only with fly-fishing opportunities in Southern California. So what follows is an overview of just the last portion, from Nevada, just north of where the Colorado begins to form the border between California and Arizona, on down to the border between California and Mexico.

The lower Colorado is a tightly controlled river. Beginning in Utah with Lake Powell, major dams manipulate every drop of water that flows toward the Gulf of California. It's even possible to get a readout of the flow patterns for the month via the Internet. The huge lakes created by these dams host primarily warmwater species such as striped bass and largemouth bass. However, you will find some trout there, albeit stocked ones. But in the river itself, trout are an afterthought. This is warmwater fly angling at its finest.

Striped bass were introduced to the Colorado River in 1962. There have been many plantings, some probably unrecorded, or the records have been lost. Although the tournament bass anglers detest stripers, the rest of the fishing public loves them. The stripers probably compete with the largemouth bass for threadfin shad, the common forage base besides bluegills and crappies, but striped bass are open-water fish that don't lurk in backwaters, like bass. There is plenty of food and habitat for both to be found in the Colorado.

Californians fishing on the Colorado River need both a California fishing license and an inexpensive reciprocal-use stamp from the neighboring state, Nevada or Arizona. The other states' river-use stamps are $3.00. Of course, you'll also need a $3.70 California striped bass stamp, since the California Fish and Game Commission has reinstated the striper-stamp program. Nevada and Arizona have several combinations of one-day and seasonal licenses for out-of-state anglers. Check with the respective states.

One thing needs to be stated up front. If you are the kind of fly angler who wants to fish with a guide, the Colorado River may not be your for you, unless you restrict yourself to the world-famous Lee's Ferry trout fishery in northern Arizona. It is not an area where you will find guides knowledgeable about the needs of a fly angler.

But that lack of local knowledge makes this part of the Colorado undiscovered country for the fly fisher, and that can be an exciting prospect. It offers the opportunity to discover new places and the challenge to develop new patterns and techniques.

The author with a schoolie-sized striped bass from Lake Havasu. Stripers this size swarm by the thousands in Havasu and other giant Colorado River reservoirs.

The author has fished parts of the lower Colorado for more than 25 years and still hasn't fished or even seen all of it. The places you find to fish and the patterns you use are likely to be as new to the old-timers as they are to you.

BULLHEAD CITY TO NEEDLES

SPECIES: Striped bass and largemouth bass. Hatchery rainbow trout from November to May.

BEST TIME: Spring and fall. Winter fishing can be good. Fishing for striped bass can be good in the middle of the summer, but the desert heat makes it tough except at night or in the very early morning and late afternoon.

FLIES: Big streamer patterns that mimic threadfin shad and other prey fish are best for stripers. Small streamers and Woolly Buggers are best for trout.

FLOAT TUBES: Not recommended in this section of the river.

LOCATION: From Los Angeles, take Interstate 15 to Barstow, then head east on Interstate 40 to Needles. Just south of there, I-40 crosses the river. From Needles, you can take Highway 95 north or south. But there are two Highway 95s. U.S. Highway 95 runs on the California side of the river, and Arizona Highway 95 parallels it on the Arizona side. Most people use Arizona 95 for north-south travel because it stays closer to the river.

Dave Cox, a longtime member of the Salt Water Fly Rodders, has fished this stretch of the river for many years. He told me recently that he thought the area was great striped bass country for the fly angler, and was amazed more fly fishers don't take advantage of it.

This portion of the river is fished via a drifting boat. There's not a lot of shore access, and the water is not wadeable in most places. Aluminum boats with reasonable horsepower are OK, but larger boats with plenty of space, freeboard, and horsepower are better. The river current is strong, and high winds often make for a rough ride.

You also need either a really good trolling motor, with lots of reserve battery power, or some sort of drag device to slow the boat below the speed of the current as it drifts. Otherwise, the fly gets yanked out of a good spot before it has a chance to drop in front of a hungry striper. The drag device known as a drift sock used on lakes won't work on rivers, since you are not being pushed through the water by the wind, but dragged along with it by the current. And because most of the river bottom in these tailrace areas (and the lakes as well) is studded with old trees, stumps, brush, and rocks, trying to drag most anchors and other heavy devices like buckets filled with cement just causes one hangup after another.

The best drag device I've heard about is one that Dave Cox and friends devised. Dave's a retired fireman, so the choice of a length of old fire hose is natural. They take several feet of hose, sew the bottom end shut, fill it with rocks, and attach a strong

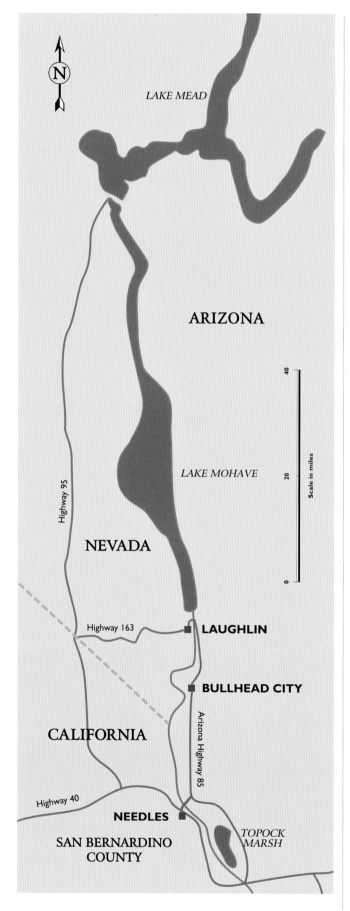

eyebolt at the top. This is tied to a stout anchor line. If you have fished conventional tackle for walleyes, steelhead, or other river sport fish, you will recognize it as a giant version of the lead-shot-filled nylon mesh tube used as a snagless sinker.

The weighted fire hose will drag on the bottom, slowing the boat. You have to experiment with weight and the amount of line you use to get the right speed. It slithers through the snags and over the rocks without getting hung up very often. The end of the drag rope has a float attached, so when a big fish hits and takes off downstream, you simply slip the line and come back for the drag later. You can work this basic rig in many parts of the river below the main dams.

Another problem boaters encounter while fishing most Colorado River tailrace areas is that the water level rises and falls during the normal cycle of hydroelectric operations. So it's entirely possible to launch, fish up or down the river for most of a day or night, then on the way back to the launch ramp knock the lower unit off your outboard on shallow rocks that used to be deep. Water releases and high water in the tailrace areas usually coincide with daily peak electrical power demand, so levels below dams are typically higher during the late afternoon and early evening, then drop during the late night and early morning.

Rods, lines, and flies for striped bass in these sections of the Colorado are usually designed to get a large streamer down into snag-filled holes where the larger bass lurk. The rods used are 8-weight or larger, with quick-sinking lines or even lead-core shooting heads. Flies are very simple. The most effective are Lefty's Deceivers, Clouser Deep Minnows, or Dan Blanton's Whistlers. Dave Cox created a big bucktail fly that is just lots of white bucktail wrapped around a body of silver tinsel. It's very effective if you can get it down. Colors should mimic threadfin shad or rainbow trout. The basic attractor colors, white or silver topped with blue or dark green, are fine.

Leaders needn't be long. From 3 to 4 feet of 10-pound test is OK for most fishing, and while 10-pound is the minimum, you could go as high as 20-pound leaders in some places. Stripers are not leader-shy. You also can use this same setup for largemouth bass in both the river and the larger lakes.

The best largemouth bass fishing is in the spring and fall, as it is in most of the lower river, although the whole area can produce fish year around. The hot months of July and August often sees the better striped bass action.

The trout in this stretch of the river are seasonal, being planted from about November through May. (When they are planted is highly dependent on water temperatures.) They can provide some good fishing for rainbows to 2 or 3 pounds around Bullhead City during the cooler months, and, of course, they draw the larger striped bass into the area. The Willow Beach National Fish Hatchery used to stock the river with trout down to Needles, and there were matching stocks by the California Department of Fish and Game until budget cutbacks and concerns about striped bass predation in 1995 put a stop to California participation.

The area is quite built up, with a number of large resorts and campgrounds, plus hotels and motels in Bullhead City and Needles. Any and all services are available, and the area is a summer recreation destination for countless boat and personal watercraft operators.

TOPOCK MARSH

SPECIES: Largemouth bass, bluegills, crappies.
BEST TIME: From the fall through midspring. Portions of the marsh are placed off-limits from October through January for waterfowl hunting.
FLIES: This is classic bass-bug water. Plan on fishing cork or deer-hair bugs on floating lines much of the time. But bring streamers and a sink-tip line, too.
FLOAT TUBES: Yes. The main, open-water portion of the marsh can be windy, but there are lots of protected backwaters to explore.
LOCATION: Just south of Needles. Take Interstate 40 to Needles, cross over the river, then go north on Arizona Highway 95.

From Needles south to the upper reaches of Lake Havasu, the primary quarry in the Colorado is a mix of striped bass and largemouth, as it is from Bullhead City down to Needles. The exception is the sprawling Topock Marsh area. Part of the Havasu National Wildlife Refuge, Topock is a birder's paradise and offers some good warmwater angling for largemouth bass, bluegills, and crappies.

Topock Marsh itself covers 4,000 acres of wetland. It's mostly shallow, averaging something like 5 feet deep. There are deeper channels that have been dredged, however, so you find a mix of water types. It is filled with drowned brush and trees and ringed with bulrushes or tules. You can use a small boat, but a float tube may be the ideal mode of transportation for the fly angler. In the middle of the summer, fishing can be fair to good for striped bass on the adjacent river, but fierce heat can limit your activities to the early and late hours of the day, or to night fishing.

Like most Colorado River angling destinations, Topock Marsh is best during spring and fall, although it can be fished right through the winter. I've never seen a giant bass from Topock, but in the spring, you can find action that seems nonstop. Some of the best takes place right after the waterfowl hunting closure is lifted on February 1. This gives anglers access to the area known as the "Glory Hole" and to other parts of the west side of the marsh that have not been fished since the previous October. Angling for crappie and bluegills improves as waters cool in October, and remains good until about the time the bass fishing picks up again.

South of I-40 is a long stretch of river known as Topock Gorge. From I-40 south to Castle Rock, the river is very popular with canoe enthusiasts and float parties in rafts. It's classic Western river country, winding through the steep cliffs and colorful desert rock. This area is also within the refuge, and camping and fires are prohibited. It tends to be good for largemouth bass, again using the drift-anchor method, plus it can offer excellent striped bass angling, as well. Dave Cox says the first couple of miles right below I-40 are very good for stripers.

This section is the place to be when Lake Havasu's striped bass make their spawning run up into the river. The hordes of fish stack up as the lake narrows, and the area from Castle Rock up to Blankenship Bend is an excellent area to hunt for stripers.

Several launch ramps are situated at Topock. Five Mile Landing is currently the only spot where you can camp right at the marsh, but Catfish Paradise at the lower end of the Marsh right off I-40 has day-use areas.

LAKE HAVASU

SPECIES: Striped bass, largemouth bass, and panfish.
BEST TIME: The fall through the spring is best for bass. Fishing for stripers is good nearly year around, except for midwinter.
FLIES: Shad patterns for both stripers and largemouths. There is some top-water action for both species, so bring some poppers.
FLOAT TUBES: Yes, but use them with caution. Havasu is a big lake (20,000 acres) with lots of high-speed boat traffic. Limit yourself to the coves and around the Bill Williams River area.
LOCATION: Take Interstate 40 to Needles, cross over the Colorado into Arizona, and take Arizona Highway 95 south to Lake Havasu City. The California-side resorts can be reached via U.S. 95.

Lake Havasu is the southernmost of the lower Colorado River's four "great lakes," Lake Powell, Lake Mead, Lake Mohave, and finally Lake Havasu, the only one that forms part of California's eastern border. The lake was created in 1938 behind Parker Dam and was intended as a storage reservoir to provide water to Southern California. It also created one of the busier recreation destinations on the river. During the "season," which is nearly the same length as the calendar year, Havasu is covered with boats, water skiers, personal watercraft, and just about every kind of fishing vessel you can imagine.

It's not uncommon to see a 12-foot aluminum boat with a small outboard flanked by a 40-foot houseboat, both being passed by a 2,000-horsepower offshore speedboat. Sleek bass boats and wildly styled runabouts and ski craft are everywhere. Spring break and summer vacations carpet the lake with boats and every other kind of floating gadget you can imagine. Havasu is a water-sports paradise, but what it may lack in solitude, it more than makes up for in the promise of excellent angling.

The lake is about 45 miles long, and when full, covers some 20,400 surface acres. Shallow by most Western reservoir standards, it averages only 50 feet, with much of the lake 30 feet deep or less—perfect for the fly angler. That translates to 211 billion gallons of clear, blue water for growing striped bass. It's in some of the West's most beautiful desert country. The river marks the convergence of the Mojave and Sonoran deserts, and it creates a spectacular riparian zone that turns to a seemingly sterile wasteland only yards from the water's edge.

That's not true, of course. Bighorn sheep, wild burros, and hardy mule deer inhabit the mountains. Gambel's quail and rabbits are abundant, along with many species of waterfowl and rap-

tors. Wildlife refuges bracket the lake. The river from Topock Marsh down to Castle Rock is within the Havasu National Wildlife Refuge, and at the south end of the lake, near Parker Dam, where the Bill Williams River runs into Havasu, there is the Bill Williams National Wildlife Area.

Stripers are just one of the warmwater species found in this long, skinny, and shallow impoundment, but they are the most prolific. Havasu has a very respectable population of large-mouth bass and a thriving bluegill and crappie fishery, but it's the almost unlimited hordes of stripers that should get fly anglers excited.

Stripers in Havasu act like stripers anywhere. They are schooling predators, hunting for pods of baitfish and then driving them like a pack of wolves pursuing a flock of sheep. The primary forage fish in Havasu is the threadfin shad. The Colorado is blessed with an abundance of these little fish, and the stripers make good use of them. In the fall, from September through the end of November, the fly of choice probably would be a small pencil popper in white or silver on a floating line, cast to stripers beating up on a school of shad. This feeding frenzy lasts for many weeks as surface waters cool. The shad move into the back bays and coves, and the stripers are not far behind.

In the summer, as well, stripers often chase schools of shad to the surface. At this time of year, using binoculars to look for gulls, grebes, and other shad-hunting birds is a popular way of finding stripers. At a distance, you may not see the splashes of

Striped bass may be the perfect warmwater fly-rod game fish. Highly predatory, they cruise in search of schools of baitfish to attack. Simple streamers will usually lead to hookups.

stripers connecting with fleeing shad, but the swirling dance of diving birds getting in on the action can be seen from a long way off.

The boils of feeding stripers means the action is fast and furious, but doesn't last long in any one spot. The preferred technique is to locate the action, get the boat close, then cut the engine to keep from spooking the stripers. One or two casts may be all you'll get, but those should account for a couple of fish. Sometimes you'll get lucky and the melee will last several minutes, with stripers from a few inches in length up to 8 or 10 pounds slashing through the panicked shad.

You always should keep a second rod handy, rigged with a sinking line and a streamer that mimics a shad. Sometimes dropping the fly down through and under the shad results in an instant hookup as a striper is fooled into thinking it's getting a bite of dead or injured shad. A sink-tip or sink-belly line will work, but since speed is of the essence, a quick-sinking line, or even a lead-core shooting head, will work better.

Leaders need not be complex, or even long. Stripers can be spooky in the shallows, but they don't seem to be aware of leaders at all. Because the average striped bass in Havasu is probably 3 or 4 pounds, you may think a light or medium tippet is

OK. Think again. The bottom of Havasu is littered with stumps and brush. A struggling striper can make short work of an 8-pound tippet in this kind of trash. Besides, while the average fish may be only a 3-pounder, the next fish that grabs your fly may weigh over 20 pounds. It's better to be safe than sorry.

Those same fast-sinking lines and stout leaders are best for the rest of the season, as well. When stripers are not on top, they often stack like cordwood on points along the lake. They face into the slow current and wait for shad and other bait to come within range. This is an important key to finding stripers on Havasu and the other large lakes on the river. These all have a perceptible current, and you need to fish them like a river, rather than a lake. The conventional-tackle anglers often drift over these points with several rods rigged with small hunks of cut anchovy to catch these fish. To duplicate this technique, the fly angler needs only to set the boat into a controlled drift using wind, current, and a good electric trolling motor to position the boat sideways and pull a streamer along the bottom.

Another technique I've learned is to "jig" the fly constantly by stripping in a few inches quickly, then releasing the line so it feeds back through the guides. This twitching motion adds life to the deep-running fly and entices stripers to hit. You can do it either while anchored or while drifting.

Flies for Lake Havasu stripers are pretty much the same as you might fish for striped bass anywhere. White is the dominant color, and solid yellow, or white/green, white/blue, or a combination of the above will all work. A Lefty's Deceiver is a natural choice, and I like a simple fly with no particular name that I got from Bob Slamal at Ski and Sport in Riverside. It's a combination of a white marabou tail and wing on a body of Jay Fair's Crystal Shuck. Think of a large Woolly Bugger with a overwing and you'll get the idea.

Another excellent fly for stripers on the river is the creation of Jack King, a former Arizona Game and Fish employee who often fished with Dave and Freddie (Winifred) Cox, the husband-and-wife team who pioneered fly fishing for Colorado River stripers during the 1960s. Called the Delta King, it's really just a simple bucktail tied very full, with a silver-tinsel chenille body and a bit of tinsel for the tail.

A few others I have not tried, but can recommend because they catch stripers anywhere, include the ALF series, Dan Blanton's Whistler, the Clouser Deep Minnow, and Dave Whitlock's Match The Minnow Shad.

The limit on striped bass in Havasu is 10 fish. Do your taste buds a big favor and take a limit home and eat them. It won't hurt the fishery a bit. In fact, it probably will improve it. The largemouth and smallmouth bass limit on the Colorado is 6 bass, with a 13-inch minimum. There is no limit on bluegills, and there is a 25-fish limit on the lake's large crappies.

For more information, you can write or call the Lake Havasu Tourism Bureau, 314 London Bridge Road, Lake Havasu City, AZ 86403, 800-2-HAVASU. Internet-enabled anglers can get more information from www.havasulanding.com or www.arizonaguide.com/lakehavasu. Don't bother looking for much in the way of fly-fishing information on any of the lower Colorado River lakes on Arizona fly-fishing web pages (www.azlink.com/~jshannon). There's lots there on trout, but nothing much on warmwater species.

For a quick source of general information on boating and fishing, try the marinas. On the California side: Black Meadow Landing, (760) 663-490; Havasu Landing, (760) 858-4593; and Havasu Palms, (760) 858-4579. On the Arizona side: Havasu Springs Resort, (520) 667-2205; Crazy Horse Campground, (520) 855-4033; Lake Havasu Marina, (520) 855-2159; Havasu State Park, (520) 855-7851; Sandpoint Marina, (520) 855-0549; and Windsor Beach, (520) 855-2784. Don't forget, though, that most of the people you talk to don't know a thing about fly fishing.

THE PARKER STRIP

SPECIES: Smallmouth bass, largemouth bass, stripers, and panfish.
BEST TIME: All year, but the spring and fall are the most productive times.
FLIES: Small streamers. Oranges and browns are especially good. The Whitlock Multi-Color Marabou Muddler is very good, as is any crayfish pattern. White shad streamers work for both largemouth bass and stripers.
FLOAT TUBES: No, not recommended for this section of the river.
LOCATION: The Parker Strip is the section of the river between Parker Dam and the California desert town of Blythe. To reach the lower end, take Interstate 10 east to Blythe. For the upper end at Parker, take I-10 to Desert Center, then Highway 177 to Highway 62 through Vidal Junction to Earp and the town of Parker.

The main species of interest to fly anglers in this stretch of the Colorado is a warmwater fish with an attitude and a comparative rarity in the dry Western states: the smallmouth bass. The smallmouth is an ideal fly-rod gamefish. Cousin to the familiar largemouth bass, the smallmouth gets its name because the back corner of the mouth does not extend rearward of the eye, as it does on the largemouth. It also is distinguished from the largemouth by its distinctive eyes and bronze coloring. The smallmouth bass is a creature of much different habitats than the largemouth as well, preferring cool, clear, and quick-flowing water to the green and weedy domain of the largemouth.

The smallmouth is a robust fish that actually does well in a variety of waters, including farm ponds, big lakes, and rivers large and small. The only requirement is that the water be cleaner and cooler than that favored by the largemouth. That prime smallmouth water can be found in the lower reaches of the Colorado River, from Parker all the way to Yuma and the Mexican border, is the result of changes brought to the river by human intervention.

Originally a sluggish, silt-laden conduit from the Rocky Mountains to the Gulf of California, the river was transformed by dams erected for hydroelectric and irrigation use. The dams slowed the river and caused it to drop its load of silt in the lake bottoms. Below the dams, the water rushing from turbines came from deep in the lakes. It then flowed crystalline and cold,

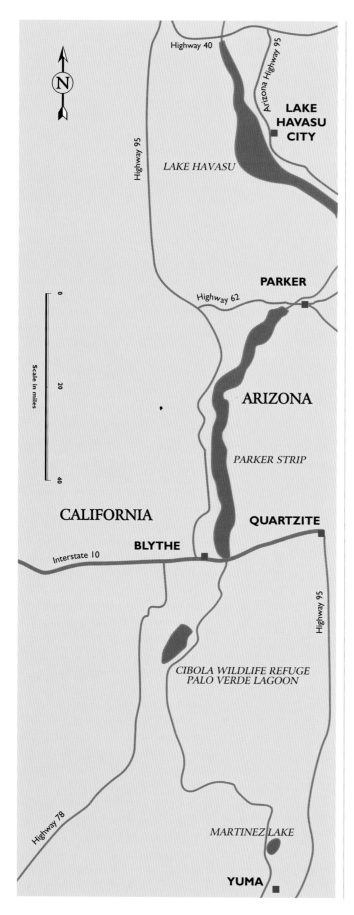

providing an ideal place to develop a sport-fishing opportunity that never existed before.

The cold waters needed one additional thing to create ideal conditions for smallmouth bass. That came in the form of flood-control measures designed to stabilize the easily eroded banks. Long stretches of the river were lined with huge chunks of riprap to keep the waters from eating away the fragile land. If there's a bottom structure or feature that suits the smallmouth bass best, it's piles of rocks. Someone whose name is now lost recognized the potential. According to Brad Jacobson, a regional fisheries specialist for the Arizona Department of Game and Fish, the Colorado River smallmouth have been there longer than the official memory of the department extends back. "They were stocked long before the records we've got."

There are smallmouth all along the main channel of the river. "Once in a great while we'll see one from one of the pot-hole lakes down in the Imperial section, but they really are a main-channel fish," said Tom Burke, a Bureau of Reclamation biologist, when I first discussed the potential for fly angling on the Colorado River with him several years ago. Tom himself is a fly angler, having tossed bass bugs at these fish quite a bit.

Most smallmouth anglers also recommend fishing the river when flows are high, which makes the launching of bass boats easier. If you drift the river in any kind of boat, casting to the shoreline rip-rap, a good pair of Polaroid sunglasses is essential. They help you pick out submerged rocks and stumps where smallmouth may lurk, but they are vitally necessary as a piece of safety equipment. The river level fluctuates widely over any 24-hour period. What was deep, safe water at sunrise may be drawn down to the level of dangerous snags, boulders, and sandbars by sunset. Tom Burke, however, told me he prefers to fish the times of minimum flow. "Wading along a shallow strip, or using something with shallow draft, like a john boat or canoe, is ideal," said Burke.

You couldn't go too far wrong if your selection of flies included a couple of crayfish patterns, but there are a number of other good patterns, as well. Any stretch of smallmouth water you can cover on foot or in a slowly drifting boat just aches to be fished with a variety of streamers. Tops on my list would be the Muddler Minnow—particularly one with a lot of orange and brown in it.

Anything that mimics the large resident dragonflies, damselflies, caddisflies, and mayflies should work, especially nymph or pupa patterns, and crossover designs like the Woolly Bugger, which can be mistaken for a small fish as well as an insect. The main requirement is that the fly exhibit life-like action. I tend to use patterns that have enough marabou in them to flutter and pulsate in the current.

Smallmouth also are much more prone to rising to hatching insects than largemouth. In that respect, their feeding actions resemble those of trout. A good collection of dry flies should include some hefty Bivisibles, downwing or Trude-pattern flies to represent caddisflies, and a few old-standby mayfly types. I still think an Adams is about as good as you can do among

Panfish, from slab-sized bluegill to nice crappie like this, are common along the Colorado. Angling at night around lighted boat docks is a good way to fill a stringer for breakfast.

these. During the time I last fished the Parker area for smallmouth, there was a constant hatch of small, grayish mayflies coming off. I saw several swirls, which could only have been mayflies being picked off by smallmouths.

Since smallmouth bass don't need the bulky, fist-sized flies that largemouth anglers favor, instead of taking your favorite bass or light saltwater rod on a river smallmouth outing, you will have more fun with what you currently use for bigger trout on still waters. An 8- or 9-foot rod matched to a 5-weight or 6-weight line is about right for most of the flies you'll fish.

Leaders can be middle-of-the-road also. A tippet testing from 4 to 6 pounds will work for most stretches of the river. Stick with a regular 9-foot leader. The clear water will require it. I'd carry two reel spools, one with a floating weight-forward or bass-taper line, the other with a sink-tip. Most of the time you'll be fishing water only 4 or 5 feet deep.

The average smallmouth taken in biologists' studies was 3 years old and in the range of one pound, although two biologists told me they did find a fair number in the 2-to-3-pound range. That seems to fall in line with the experiences of most of the anglers who search for smallmouth bass on the river.

The latest Arizona record smallmouth is 5-pounds and just under 3 ounces, caught in the Parker area by Gene Albers of Fontana, California. The old record was a very respectable 4-pound-plus fish caught by Gene McKinny of Yuma, Arizona. In September, 1980, McKinny was fishing the Taylor Lake portion of the river, near Picacho State Recreation Area on the California side, when he hooked and landed this long-standing record fish.

South of Blythe, there is a beautiful stretch of river that includes the Cibola National Wildlife Refuge, the Imperial National Wildlife Refuge, and hundreds of backwater "lakes" that hold largemouth bass. This would not seem to be good smallmouth water, and it is true that there isn't much of the classic riprap rock cover. However, that hasn't kept people from catching some very nice smallmouths here, in the areas where those fish can thrive.

A part of the Colorado that's recently come to light as a potential quality smallmouth fishery is the section just above Palo Verde Dam near Blythe. A few years ago, the Blythe Bass Club held a local bass tournament in the area above the dam, and the big smallmouth of the tournament weighed nearly 3 pounds. The winner had a 5-fish stringer weighing 9 pounds, every one a smallmouth.

Both Blythe and Parker are small towns, but they have all the services and camping facilities you'll need. This stretch of the river is primarily a water playground for boaters and water skiers. You'll find launch ramps, marinas, service stations, and

everything else you'll need for fishing except fly shops.

One curious bit of fishing you might find interesting is angling for bass and bluegills along the many large agricultural canals in the area. I've caught smallmouths, tilapias, and bluegills in man-made waterways. The setting isn't fancy, but they can be offer surprisingly good fishing.

ARIZONA'S "EVERGLADES"

SPECIES: Primarily largemouth bass, plus smallmouths. There is fair striped bass fishing, as well as excellent angling for bluegills and crappies.

BEST TIME: The early spring and late fall, but the area is fishable anytime.

FLIES: Shad imitations, crayfish patterns, bass bugs, and poppers for bass. Larger streamers for striped bass. Take a small box of dry flies, nymphs, and small cork bugs for panfish.

FLOAT TUBES: Yes. The hundreds of pothole lakes and backwater lagoons offer some of the best float-tube fishing on the river.

LOCATION: Take Interstate 10 east to Blythe. The Palo Verde area and Cibola National Wildlife Refuge offer some very good fishing on the California side. Use Highway 78 south. To reach Martinez Lake and the Imperial Wildlife Refuge, cross the river on I-10, then turn south on Arizona 95 at Quartzite.

From the California border town of Blythe south to the city of Yuma in Arizona, the weedy back bays, meandering side channels, and tule-ringed pothole lakes off the main channel of

Shallow marshes, like this one at Topock, near the town of Needles, offer exceptional angling for panfish, largemouth bass, and sometimes even striped bass.

the Colorado River give fly-rod bass anglers access to some of the West's best bass fishing. This is true largemouth bass country.

When Imperial Dam just north of Yuma was finished in 1935, the Colorado flooded into desert canyons and gullies, creating hundreds of winding channels, hidden "lakes," and seep ponds or potholes. Most are not really lakes, simply openings in the vast network of plant life where the water depth stops growth. The majority are not isolated from each other by dry land, and fish can swim through the tules to reach the main river and other potholes.

Those potholes that are landlocked usually have been stocked by earlier generations of anglers. The smaller potholes in the dense tules are best fished with a float tube, pram, or johnboat. Excursions up or down the river usually mean renting or bringing a power boat. A good way to fish the area is to go in a group, rent or bring a pontoon boat to serve as a floating base, and use float tubes.

With a float tube, you have access to many spots where you may have to walk and crash your way through waist-deep water and tules for yards to reach a "lake." The reward is that your destination may not have been fished for years, or decades—or ever. The growth patterns of the aquatic vegetation and changes in river flows constantly remake much of the area, and a multi-agency state and federal task group is busy rebuilding some of the backwater region to improve fishing and angling access.

Starting just south of Blythe, the first prime area for angling is the Palo Verde Lagoon near the farming communities of Ripley and Palo Verde. This gets relatively little fishing pressure and can produce some very nice bass in the spring months and again in the fall. You can see most of the fishing spots on the AAA map Guide to the Colorado River and a lot more detail on Fish-n-Map's Lower Colorado River (Parker to Yuma) map.

Another excellent resource is a small map booklet put out by the California Department of Boating and Waterways. Called *A Boating Trail Guide to the Colorado River*, it is designed for canoe travelers and maps all the camps, backwaters, and other items of interest to boaters and anglers. (See the Appendix for addresses.)

South of Palo Verde Lagoon is the Cibola National Wildlife Refuge, a 17,000-acre sanctuary for migratory birds. Like Topock Marsh, portions of Cibola are closed from early September to mid-March for wintering migratory birds, but fishing is permitted within portions of the refuge and in the main river channel.

Just south of Cibola, the Colorado enters the upper reaches of the Imperial National Wildlife Refuge. Even larger than Cibola, the Imperial refuge covers both sides of the river for many miles and encloses over 25,000 acres. Much of the best backwater bass angling takes place in the 30 or so miles of the Colorado above Imperial Dam. The hub of angling activity is found at the resort of Martinez Lake on the Arizona side of the river.

Fishing here can be an unusual experience. You can fish all day long without seeing another angler, yet hear the sounds of boat traffic and voices from other anglers and water skiers on the main river often just a few yards away. You also can be awakened by the thump of heavy artillery or the rattlesnake snarl of a 25-millimeter chain gun in the distance. Martinez Lake is accessed through the U.S. Army Yuma Proving Grounds, and such sounds are common during weekdays.

Since there are both tiny potholes and big, open areas, almost all flies, fly-fishing lines, and fishing tactics will work somewhere here. However, most fly fishers will probably opt for a floating line and bass bugs. The dense tules and brush ringing the shores of all these lakes makes accurate casting a must, and foam or cork bugs last longer among the saw-blade tule stems than hair bugs.

Besides fishing poppers, another prime tactic for fly rodders is to reproduce the bass pro's technique of flipping a plastic worm into tiny pockets at the base of the shore cover. You can do this with a sink-tip line or a floater with an 18-inch section of lead-core line added. Cast a Whitlock Eelworm or the like directly at the base of the brush. Most of the bass are not giants, but there are thousands per mile, and there are enough 5-pound and 6-

pound fish to keep things very interesting. Many of the small-to-medium bass lurk well back inside the brush that forms the edges of the potholes, but remember that the visible growth may be standing in 3 or 4 feet of water, and the fish can retreat as far back as they like.

Another good tactic is casting to the many clumps of drowned trees that line the deeper center channels of these pothole lakes. Early and late in the day, try a floating line and a popper, but from midmorning through midafternoon, a full-sinking line and a bottom-crawling fly will produce better. It's worth noting that the current Arizona Colorado River record largemouth bass of 16 pounds, 14 ounces was caught in the Yuma area.

Martinez Resort features lodging in cabins and modern house trailers, an RV park, and primitive camping areas for self-contained campers and trailers. Almost next door is Fisher's Landing, which also has a marina, camping, and an RV park with hookups and a boat shop. Fisher's has a small store and serves breakfast in their club. Martinez has a restaurant that opens later in the day for lunch and dinner. Both have bars for evening socializing.

Dock space and boat launching are available both at Martinez and Fisher's Landing, with boat rentals available at Martinez. In addition to fishing, hunting, and water-skiing on the main river, other attractions include canoe float trips, guided boat tours through some of the most spectacular scenery on the river, and fishing guide services.

For fly anglers with an urge to visit new waters, the laid-back atmosphere of Martinez and Fishers is more like the 1950s than the beginning of the twenty-first century. The fishing is excellent, the water and surrounding desert are wildly beautiful, and the ambiance is unique.

Contact Martinez Lake Resort, Star Route #4, Box 41, Martinez Lake, AZ 85365, (520) 783-9589, or 1-800-876-7004 for reservations. Fisher's Landing right next door has a mini-mart (520) 782-7049, and their boat shop number is (520) 343-2776. Fisher's Landing Campground, which has both primitive and RV hookup sites, is (520) 539-9495. One thing you won't find is a fly-fishing guide in the area. Wally Wolfe, (520) 783-9589, is the local bass guide. He can put you on the right track for bass. The best map of the area for anglers is the Lower Colorado River (Parker to Yuma) offered by Fish-n-Map.

Below Martinez, the Colorado continues on to the California-Mexico border. More potholes, sloughs, and good bass fishing occur along the main river channel all the way past Senator Wash Reservoir and Mittry Lake to behind Laguna Dam. If you are feeling a bit jaded in your pursuit of Southern California's many sport-fish species, spend a little time on the largest of the Southland's waterways. The Colorado is a unique and fascinating destination that is only a half-day from most Southern California cities.

CHAPTER NINE

A FEW SURPRISES

IN ADDITION TO THE RESERVOIRS, LAKES, AND streams already discussed, there are a few places that used to be or might become fly-fishing destinations, but that don't quite fit the ideal of the typical fly angler's fishing spot. The Salton Sea is one such place. In its heyday, it was a definite destination for fly anglers who wanted to tangle with a big orangemouth corvina without traveling to Mexico. After languishing for more than a decade and completely dropping off the map of fly-fishing attractions, it appears to be making a comeback. And a couple of the smaller lakes listed in this chapter are not what you would call hot destinations, yet they have allowed fly anglers to set International Game Fish Association records for largemouth bass. In fact, one quite interesting destination doesn't even exist yet. That's where we'll start.

THE EASTSIDE RESERVOIR PROJECT

SPECIES: Rainbow, brown, and lake trout. Largemouth, smallmouth, and spotted bass, bluegills, crappies, and redear sunfish.
BEST TIME: Year-round.
FLIES: Caddisfly and attractor patterns for trout. Bass bugs and minnow imitations for warmwater bass and panfish. Shad-style streamers for everything.
FLOAT TUBES: Regulations for float tubing and boating are unknown at this time.
LOCATION: Domenigoni Valley, about 4 miles southwest of Hemet.

In yet another attempt to keep up with the development boom that seems to be paving over or building on every last inch of the southern half of California, the Metropolitan Water District is building another giant water-storage and transfer reservoir. The numbers are mind-boggling. More than ninety million cubic yards of clay, sand, and rock will be used to create what the DWP is claiming will be the largest earth-fill dam project in the United States. They started taking rock for the two dams in 1995, and shortly after the millennium there should be enough water in the lake for angling.

The Eastside Reservoir (which might wind up being named Domenigoni, for the valley and the family of the same name) will have a surface area of 4,500 acres. It will be 4.5 miles long, more than 2 miles wide, and between 160 and 260 feet deep. It will be the largest reservoir in Southern California, and the extreme depth is what should set this twenty-first-century fishery apart from the rest of the still waters in the Southland.

According to DFG biologist Mike Giusti, who is working the problem of what kind of fish to stock in this new lake, the depth creates a "two-story fishery," with shallows capable of supporting both warmwater fish like crappies, bluegills, bass, and

Haiwee Reservoir (actually two reservoirs under one name), is almost unknown to fly fishers, yet offers good angling for trout and bass. Much of these reservoirs is wadeable.

catfish, and depths cold enough to provide sanctuary for trout.

"We have sought input from the public, and so far about 90 percent of the public seem to want some kind of bass," Giusti told me in late 1997. "We are looking at three different bass, Florida-strain largemouths, spotted bass, and smallmouth bass. We would probably stock Florida largemouths and smallmouth bass initially, then introduce the spots at a later date. We would also stock, bluegills, redear sunfish, and crappies."

Given the political clout of the organized bass clubs (They have a semi-official status within the Warmwater Fishery Board and the Southern California Bass Council) this mix of bass is not surprising, nor is it necessarily a bad idea. Fly fishing for bass is a wonderful sport, and while there are lots of largemouth bass lakes, the area has a distinct shortage of smallmouth and spotted bass waters. Both of these bass have reputations for being outstanding fly-rod fish.

Giusti also noted that a lot of people want to see trout in the Eastside Reservoir. Because of the depth of the reservoir, we could have several species of resident wild trout along with the bass, not just hatchery rainbows tossed into the lake during the winter months.

"We are looking at the idea of a diverse coldwater fishery with possibly rainbow or brown trout, kokanee salmon, silver salmon, and even lake trout," Giusti suggested. "I don't know if we can pull this off, but I would like to try. The lake trout are perhaps the best bet for an experiment of this type, since they could reproduce in the reservoir." The other trout species require streams and spawning gravel of certain sizes to be successful. Lake trout can spawn on a lake bottom. "It would be a really unique fishery for Southern California," Giusti said.

"Unique" is right. From the middle of the winter on into early spring, the surface temperatures would be cold enough to bring the lake trout into the shallows, where fly anglers might have a chance to fight a giant trout without traveling north. Lake trout grow to amazing size. I think it might be possible to hook a trout of 25 pounds or more a few years into the twenty-first century if Giusti gets his way.

Brown trout also are an exciting possibility for the Eastside Reservoir. Many of the local streams have browns, but there currently is no lake in Southern California with a hardy population of brown trout. Lake Arrowhead has some browns, but access is difficult. Lake Gregory was stocked with browns, but they've shown little progress. I remember Silverwood when you had a better than average chance of catching a 5-pound brown on any given day, and while such a fishery must be supported by stocking, browns in such a large and deep lake would soon take on the habits of wild fish.

One thing neither the DFG nor the bass anglers want is for the lake to fall victim to an invasion of striped bass. According to Giusti, efforts will be made to construct some kind of electric or electronic fence to keep stripers out. However, he also believes the arrival of striped bass via water from the Colorado River inevitably will happen at some point in the future.

At this time, ideas for recreational facilities are still being refined, but you can expect that the Eastside Reservoir will have camp facilities, launch ramps, and marinas, sailing, boating (unfortunately including water skiing and personal watercraft), and fishing. At the time this chapter was finalized, there were no phone numbers or other ways of getting information.

THE SALTON SEA

SPECIES: Orangemouth corvinas, sargos, croakers, tilapias,

BEST TIME: The hotter the weather, the better the fishing. The best fishing usually is in midsummer.

FLIES: Streamers and popping bugs. Corvinas like bright colors

FLOAT TUBES: Yes. Much of the shore is shallow flats that also can be waded.

LOCATION: The Salton Sea is approximately 140 miles southeast of Los Angeles. Go east on Highway 60 to Coachella, then take Highway 111 to the north-shore resorts, or Highway 86 to the south-shore resorts.

The Salton Sea may be the most improbable fishery in a state where the improbable hardly draws a raised eyebrow. First, it is an accident. It did not exist until a 1905 flood damaged an irrigation dam and canal near Yuma. The flood of water into the dry valley lasted for two years, forming a shallow, salty inland sea some 20 miles wide and 45 miles long. Evaporation reduced the original size. It's now 35 miles in length, and, depending on water flows, some 15 miles across. There are several resorts and marinas on each shore, plus a state park with recreational facilities.

For the first forty-five years of its life, the Salton Sea was nothing more than California's largest puddle, but in the early 1950s, the California Department of Fish and Game decided to stock it with fish that would tolerate the high salinity. They began transplanting orangemouth corvinas, sargos, and croakers from the Gulf of California, and later, tilapias that were stocked in the canals that feed the sea created another good fishery when they moved into the sea itself. Salton Sea sportfish populations have been self-sustaining since 1956, when the last fish taken from Mexican waters was stocked.

Within just a few years, the fishing went from zero to hero. Anglers flocked to the sea, and fly fishers discovered they could catch corvinas averaging 10 pounds without too much trouble. The number of fly anglers fishing the Salton Sea never was large in the 1960s and 1970s, but those who got in on the action were simply awed by the fantastic fishing they found. The husband-and-wife duo of Dave and Freddie Cox, well-known casting instructors and striper anglers, used to fish the sea a lot. To hear Dave tell it, the fishing was as good as it gets.

"It was unbelievable during the late 1950s and into the 1960s," Dave laughed. "You could wade out at Corvina Beach and catch 20-pound corvina on flies. Actually, a 7 or 8-pound fish was about the average size, and there were some fish in the sea we just never stopped, so I don't know how big they were."

The record there is something like 37 pounds. I have no idea what the largest fly-rod-caught Salton Sea corvina is, and today you could still catch corvina to 15 or 20 pounds, but it's likely the average corvina would tip the scales at the 5-pound mark.

Cox told me he thought that in addition to the corvinas, sargos, and croakers, the DFG also planted totuavas, a member of the corvina family that averages 35 to 100 pounds, with some to 250 pounds.

"The totuavas didn't reproduce, I think," he said, "but the ones planted grew to adult size. They never found a dead one, and there were lots of stories about big fish you couldn't stop. I pulled in an 8-pound corvina that had teeth marks clear up by the gills. Something had gotten that whole corvina in its mouth.

"We used a fly we called a Freddie Green. It was just a bucktail on a 4/0 to 2/0 hook. We used white bucktail on the bottom, green on top and with a bit of Mylar and twelve or fifteen peacock herls on top. It didn't really matter—when the bite was on at the sea, they would hit anything. We used to fish the Golden Comet salmon fly when they got touchy. The fishing is very good at night, but the Salton Sea is a spooky place to fish in the dark. The crack of dawn and the evening are the best times of day. The best fishing months are the midsummer ones, so fishing is restricted to early and late because of the temperatures."

He noted that some fly fishers used to fish out of inner tubes, particularly in the hot weather as a means of staying cool. He said that areas like North Shore, Mecca Beach, or Corvina Beach are ideal for fly fishers. These are all on the north shore of the sea.

"My favorites are Mecca and Corvina Beach," Cox suggested. "I caught a 4-pound tilapia on a fly down there once. It's real shallow wading there. You can wade out a quarter of a mile and still only be up to your knees. It's got kind of a slippery bottom. I've heard stories of guys wading down there getting bit on the belt buckle. When they are feeding, you could tie a rock on a string and get a strike. Corvina have a set of teeth you won't forget. I think they would hit a big popper, too, but I never tried it. You can sight fish for corvina at times. If a school of corvinas is busting up tilapias you can see that action and cast to those fish. They will also push up schools of little croakers at times. If you can find schools of croakers near the surface, there will be corvinas under them."

In those days, the Coxes and other anglers working the sea usually fished lead-core shooting-head systems. "We would run a 22-foot head backed up by Cobra flat mono so you could fish a lot of water. We even used it while wading in the shallows to get the fly right on the bottom. We also used Hi-D sinking heads. Sometimes sink-tips."

Dick Gaumer, a freelance writer and former editor of *Angler* magazine, agreed the fly fishing at the Salton Sea was the stuff of legends. He thinks he might have been among the first to cast a fly over corvina at the sea.

"It was fabulous, I used to fish it every weekend. I had a little car-top boat. We would pull the boat out on a point and fish,"

Bill Murphy with a huge Lake Wohlford largemouth bass. Fish of this size can sometimes be caught by fly anglers who master the art of fishing with sinking lines.

Gaumer remembers. "I would fish both flies and conventional tackle, even live mudsuckers at times. We would stay in Indio. I think I was one of the first guys to catch a corvina on a fly. That was probably 1960. I didn't know what to tie, but I did know that corvina liked a lot of bright colors, so I tied up some large Mickey Finn streamers, and that's what I caught my first corvina on. The fish weighed 17 pounds. I caught it wading along the shore."

The fishing got into trouble in the mid-1980s. A variety of misfortunes started chasing anglers away. Avian botulism killed millions of waterfowl in various outbreaks over the years. And because the Salton Sea has no outlet, it becomes a settling basin for all the agricultural runoff from the crops grown in the Imperial Valley. As time went by, deposited salts and metals built up, and in the 1980s, there were all kinds of scare stories about the imminent death of the sea. A lot of it was sloppy journalism, but it drove anglers away from the sea in great numbers.

Today, The Salton Sea may be the most misunderstood fishery in the West, at least among fly-rod anglers. Many are convinced there are no fish in the Salton Sea, while the conventional-tackle anglers continue to fish the Sea and score on corvina. While I was discussing the fishing with Steve Horvath, head of the Salton Sea State Recreation Area, a guy checked in with a 19-pound corvina. A talk with the ranger at Red Hill Marina also revealed good fishing in the fall of 1997, with the average corvina running around 5 to 9 pounds. The 37-pound state record was caught in 1988, about the time everybody decided the sea was dead.

More recently, efforts to fix the sea's problems and bring it back have gotten underway, notably by the Salton Sea Authority, which has the political clout to initiate programs and secure funding for them. The fishery, however, has returned on its own, and in a big way. This comeback most probably results from several years of benign neglect. Anglers and biologists left the fish alone, and after several years of drought, fresh water brought by rain has offset the salinity somewhat, allowing some reproduction by the corvina. The tilapias have reproduced in the millions in recent years, and corvina are not only plentiful, but getting larger, mostly as a result of consuming huge numbers of tilapias. The Salton Sea is again fertile ground for fly fishers to explore.

The Salton Sea has plenty of access for anglers. There are a half-dozen marinas, camping facilities that range from fancy to primitive, and motels in Indio. The other small communities of Niland, Westmoreland, Salton City, and Brawley have some services, mostly gas and food.

Launching fees for boats vary from $9.00 at some of the private launch ramps to free at the Imperial County parks. The county parks number is (760) 339-4384. The number for the Salton Sea State Recreation Area on the north shore is (760) 393-3052. Reservations for camping there are made through DESTINET at (800) 444-7275.

The sea is open to fishing 24 hours a day. There is no limit on tilapias, croakers, and sargos. Corvinas have a 5-fish limit.

LAKE ISABELLA

SPECIES: Rainbow trout, largemouth bass, crappies, bluegills, and chinook salmon.

BEST TIME: The spring and summer are best for bass. The winter and spring are best for trout and salmon.

FLIES: This is not a lake for bass bugs. Try sinking lines and streamers for bass. The chinook salmon should be feeding on shad, so try small white streamers. For trout, you can't go wrong with a Woolly Bugger or any of a variety of nymphs.

FLOAT TUBES: Yes. Stay within 100 feet of the shore. Isabella is a large lake with much high-speed boat traffic, and the wind can be dangerous, as well.

LOCATION: Isabella is 160 miles north of Los Angeles. Take Interstate 5 north to Wheeler Ridge, then go right on the Lake Isabella/Arvin exit. Follow Highway 184 (Wheeler Ridge Road) to Highway 178, then drive 41 miles up the lower Kern River to the lake. From the Inland Empire, take Highway 395 north to Inyokern, then switch back south on Highway 14 a few miles to Highway 178.

Isabella, a Y-shaped reservoir at the junction of two forks of the Kern River, lies in the Sierra foothills east of Bakersfield. It is Southern California's largest lake, with a capacity of 11,400 surface acres and 570,000 acre-feet of water storage. Isabella been filled nearly to capacity only three times in thirty years. Anglers who have fished the lake would think normal is around 350,000 acre-feet.

Built in the early 1950s as a flood-control measure, it handles runoff from 2,093 square miles of mountains. Once filled, Isabella quickly became a fishing hot spot for many species. Panfishing was big business, with tremendous schools of crappies breeding and eating minnows in the brush and trees that ringed the lake. One-hundred-fish days were common. Heck, 100-fish hours were not unheard-of!

I remember fishing the tree line along the old river channel by the county airport in the spring of 1982. My wife and I launched our flat-bottomed johnboat at Camp 9 on a particularly windless day, motored to the trees, and began catching crappies as fast as we could get a fly into the green water. The bluegill fishing was nearly as good. In the winter, a vigorous trout-stocking program produced rainbows to 9 pounds, 10 ounces and brown trout to 22 pounds, 15 ounces. Not only that, Isabella was becoming known as a great place to drown stink baits for fast-growing channel catfish.

If there was a single drawback to this fantastic fishing, it was the afternoon winds.

Mornings often were utterly calm, with the whole lake looking like a plate of glass. Just after noon, on most days, the winds would spring up, quickly ripping the surface into white-caps. The whole thing happened so swiftly, and the waves generated were so intense, that boats sank and people drowned nearly every year. The Kern County Parks and Recreation Department installed a set of towers visible from the entire lake. These had lights to tell boaters when the lake was becoming dangerous. They backed up this warning system with a lake patrol and closed the lake to all boat traffic when the winds were worst. That's no longer the case. The lights are there, and in use, but the lake closures have stopped.

Isabella stepped on the trophy largemouth bass stage in a dramatic debut in the mid-1980s with a string of record catches. Northern-strain largemouth had been placed in the lake shortly after it filled, and fishing was fair to good from the start. What changed the picture was the introduction of Florida-strain bass in 1972.

Excellent habitat filled with brush and trees, a fantastic forage base of threadfin shad, hitch, baby crappies and bluegills, and the accelerated growth rate of Florida and Florida-northern hybrid bass all combined to cause a bass explosion. The lake record was broken four times between 1982 and 1983, with fish of 13 pounds, 9 ounces, 16 pounds, 9 ounces, 18 pounds, 13 ounces, and 18 pounds, 14 ounces caught. Two more 18-pound bass were taken in 1985. In that year, Steve and Jerry Beasley, fishing in January, caught two limits in one day that totaled 107 pounds, 7 ounces.

Unfortunately, this ideal state of affairs ended with the statewide drought of the late 1980s. As the lake began to shrink, the bass fishing got tougher. The receding water eliminated much of the productive shoreline habitat, and the bass, bluegill, and crappie populations crashed. A return to more normal water levels, however, has turned this fishery around. This has been aided by a number of habitat programs carried out by local anglers and the DFG. Until we get into another prolonged drought cycle, Isabella should be an excellent lake for the bass and panfish angler.

In early 1996, Isabella got a whole new fishery. Chinook salmon were introduced.

Chinook are a put-and-take fish in most waters. Very few lakes will develop any kind of reproducing population. However Isabella just might be able to do so because the Kern River enters at the north end of the lake. People are definitely catching chinooks at Isabella. They were probably 9 or 10 inches long when they first started to show in angler's live wells, but in the past year or so, the size has moved up to fish of 13 to 14 inches. They are growing very well.

At Isabella, the chinooks will be second fiddle to the trout until they start reaching larger sizes, which might be something like 7 to 9 pounds at maturity. The chinooks are in Isabella to reduce the population of the larger threadfin shad. The big shad run as large as 7 or 8 inches, and the biologists hope the chinooks will eliminate the bigger fish.

Isabella is a relatively developed area. The small towns of Kernville, Wofford Heights, and other, even smaller spots have all the services you need except for a full-service fly shop. There are public launch ramps around the lake, and camping is available. For more information, call the Kern Valley Visitor's Council, (760) 379-5646, or the Kernville Chamber of Commerce, 376-2629. The lake has three major marinas. Dean's North Fork, (760) 376-1812; French Gulch, (760) 379-8774; and Kern Valley, (760) 379-1634.

The Kern River below Isabella also has some fair to good trout fishing, and some smallmouth bass fishing. This is the only river with smallmouth in Southern California as far as I know, except for a bit of the Santa Ynez River in Santa Barbara County. Above Isabella, the Kern is a beautiful, full-sized river with boulders and pools the size of houses. This is a summer stream. Spring runoff waters can leave the river high and dangerous to wade. General regulations apply from Kernville north to the Johnsondale Bridge, then special regulations take over. This section is open from the last Saturday in April to November 15 with a two-trout limit, with a 14-inch minimum size, artificial lures with barbless hooks only. From November 16 to the last Saturday in April, the section is catch-and-release only.

THE HAIWEE RESERVOIRS

SPECIES: Rainbow and brown trout, smallmouth and largemouth bass.
BEST TIME: Best in the spring and fall.
FLIES: Dry flies and nymphs for trout. Big dry flies and nymphs for smallmouths, streamers and bass bugs for largemouths. Woolly Buggers work for everything.
FLOAT TUBES: Yes. Also, much of the shore line is wadeable.
LOCATION: Haiwee (actually two reservoirs) is just off Highway 395. From Los Angeles, take Interstate 5 to Highway 14 past Edwards Air Force Base. Highway 14 joins Highway 395 north at Inyokern-Ridgecrest. From Orange County and the Inland Empire cities, take I-15 through the Cajon Pass to Highway 395 near Hesperia and Victorville. Either way, the trip is around 180 miles. The reservoirs lie in a scenic canyon 8 miles north of Coso Junction and 23 miles south of Lone Pine. There are four entrance roads to the two reservoirs. Watch for signs.

Haiwee? What the heck is Haiwee? Actually, you shouldn't be all that surprised if you haven't heard of Haiwee Reservoir. It's part of the Los Angeles Department of Water and Power aqueduct system that brings (some Owens Valley residents would say "steals") water from the Owens Valley region of the eastern Sierra. It's also the water farthest north in this guide book. It's a high-desert fishery that's been off the radar screens of most Southern California fly anglers, but it has some big trout, and it deserves to be better known.

The name "Haiwee" is Paiute. It probably means "Dove," but the kindly female voice on the phone from the Eastern California Museum in Independence told me she wouldn't swear to it. Depending on whom you ask, the correct pronunciation is either "Hay-Way" or "Hi-Wee."

Haiwee is a double reservoir: North Haiwee is approximately 600 surface acres, and South Haiwee is larger at 800 surface acres. There are four anglers' access points with small parking lots, two for each reservoir. From south to north, they are South Haiwee, Haiwee Canyon Road, Lakeview Drive, and North Haiwee Road. The last time I was there, only Lakeview Road was marked with a sign on Highway 395, but that's one of the best places to fish anyhow. The others won't take much hunting to locate.

Only one of the four roads is paved, but since they are all quite short (less than a mile on average) and reasonably well maintained, any vehicle will suffice. Only Lakeview Drive on the lower end of North Haiwee gets you really close to the water. Float-tube anglers will have to carry tubes and equipment a fair distance through narrow walk-through gates and down dirt roads to reach the water at two of the other entrances. The northernmost at North Haiwee Road requires you to descend a steel stairway and cross the aqueduct before scrambling up a bank to reach the actual lake.

Under DWP regulations, body contact with the water is not allowed. You can't wade or tube wet—full chest waders are required. This can be a bit of a problem in the heat of summer when you are hiking a mile or two to get at a favorite spot, but the benefit of no body contact is the total absence of swimmers, water skiers, and personal watercraft to bother you.

"I fish both Upper and Lower Haiwee, and one recent year we caught and released in excess of 2,000 bass," said Bob Hayner. "I wade and fish, instead of float tubing. The upper lake is more pristine and has lots of water that can be waded. There are parking areas and plenty of miles in between, so anglers should be aware they have to hoof it some to reach the good fishing—each reservoir is about 3 miles long."

A locksmith from Lone Pine, Hayner is the president of the Owens Valley Warm Water Fishing Association, a group of anglers who include fly fishers, Sierra Club members, avid spin-fishing trout anglers, bass anglers, Audubon Society people, members of the Inyo County Board of Supervisors, Inyo Water Department personnel, Sheriff's Department employees, and at least one member who is a high-profile professional bass tournament angler. It was the association that got Haiwee opened to public fishing access, overcoming the DWP's reluctance.

While the emphasis from the Warm Water Association is on the bass in Haiwee (it has both largemouths and smallmouths) and on conventional-tackle angling, Haiwee also is an excellent trout fishery. It is "stocked" via the California Aqueduct, and both rainbows and browns prowl the reservoirs.

Frances Pedneau, a contractor in Lone Pine and a Warm Water Association member, told me he's heard of browns weighing up to 8 pounds coming from Haiwee and said that one year an angler from the Antelope Valley Fly Rodders took a 10-pound rainbow. He also noted that Haiwee has produced largemouth bass near the 10-pound mark.

"Haiwee is still predominantly a conventional-tackle fishery," said Chuck Newmyer. "There are more and more fly anglers finding out about the lake, but it's still relatively unknown." Newmyer owns the High Sierra Fly Fisher shop in the desert community of Ridgecrest and is a member of the Aguabonita Fly Fishers. Some might wonder at a fly-fishing club in the middle of the Mojave Desert, but while there isn't much extra water there, Lake Isabella and the Kern river lie to the west, and the Lower Owens River, Lake Crowley, Hot Creek, and many other Sierra waters—Haiwee included—are only an hour or two drive from this small desert community. The shop is a good stopping place to get information on Haiwee, Kennedy Meadows, Lake Isabella, and other waters in the area.

There's a rest stop at Coso Junction, with a store and restaurant, but there are no services at Haiwee. You can find a gas station, a small restaurant, and a motel above Haiwee at Olancha, but the first real town is Lone Pine, about 30 miles north of Haiwee. There you'll find tackle shops, good food and lodging, and plenty of campgrounds. Farther north are the familiar towns of Independence, Big Pine, and Bishop. For recommendations on fishing Haiwee and other information, call the Lone Pine Chamber of Commerce, (760) 876-4444 (ask them for a copy of the Lone Pine Visitor's Guide); Slater's Sporting Goods, (760) 876-5020; the Owens Valley Warm Water Fishing Association (Bob Hayner), (760) 876-5402; the Bureau of Land Management Ridgecrest Office, (760) 375-7125; the Bureau of Land Management Bishop Office, (760) 872-4881; the Interagency Visitor's Center (760) 876-6222; or High Sierra Fly Fisher in Ridgecrest, (760) 375-5810.

Haiwee is open year around for bass angling, with a 2-fish limit and a 12-inch minimum length. The rules recently were changed to allow trout fishing year around, as well. The limit for trout is five daily, ten in possession. The Department of Water and Power has a nice little brochure about Haiwee, which you can get from their Bishop office at 300 Mandich Street, Bishop, CA 93514, (760) 872-1104.

LAKE WOHLFORD

SPECIES: Largemouth bass, panfish, and, in the winter, trout.
BEST TIME: From early April until the end of the season in September for bass. From December to May for put-and-take trout.
FLIES: Shad-colored poppers on floating lines, Marabou Muddlers, streamers, and big nymphs fished on sink-tip lines. For planted trout in the winter, try bright attractor patterns and Woolly Buggers.
FLOAT TUBES: Yes. Private boats are permitted and rental boats are available.
LOCATION: Lake Wohlford is located in Escondido, about 40 miles from downtown San Diego and 114 miles from Los Angeles. Take Interstate 15 to Escondido, then go east on Valley Parkway to the Lake Wohlford turnoff. From there, it is approximately a mile and a half to lake Wohlford Resort.

Most of the fine bass lakes in San Diego County are operated by the City of San Diego, but Lake Wohlford is operated by the Escondido Parks and Recreation Department. A modest 146-surface-acre reservoir situated in the oak-dotted foothills on the northeast side of Escondido, a growing city in the upper end of the county. Wohlford is an old reservoir, originally built in 1895 and then known as Bear Valley Reservoir. It was renamed Wohlford in 1924 when the dam height was raised to create the lake that exists today.

The lake has had bass and has been stocked with trout since the early 1950s, but in 1961, Florida-strain largemouth from Upper Otay were transplanted into Wohlford. The descendants of these bass, probably hybridized with northern-strain fish, have produced a good population of chunky, well-conditioned bass. The lake record is a 19-pound, 3-ounce fish taken in 1966, and Wohlford turns out bass in the that weigh in the middle teens almost every year—sometimes several in one year.

Despite that, Wohlford is known by local anglers as a challenging lake that can be quite tough to master. Two things make the lake a difficult place to figure out: the place the lake was built and its primary water source. Wohlford was not built by damming an existing stream. Instead, a canyon was chosen, the dam was built, and then water was redirected to the new reservoir via a canal. This means there is not a deep-water main channel in the lake, only a flat, nearly featureless bottom in the deepest areas. Wohlford has fair to good shoreline structure and lots of rocks in the shallows when the water level is up, but low water means that a lot of good structure is out of the water and unavailable to the bass. In low-water conditions, they suspend over featureless bottoms.

Wohlford gets runoff rain water from Lake Henshaw to the north, and in many years, this cold influx arrives in March, just as other bass lakes start waking up. This postpones the onset of the spring bass action by several weeks. Often the best fishing is not in March, but in April and May, when other local lakes are beginning to slow.

Until recently, the Escondido Parks and Recreation Department did not permit float tubing in Lake Wohlford. At the time of this writing, float-tube anglers are welcome on a trial basis. Regulations for tubers are about the same as for other San Diego area lakes. Tubers must wear full waders to eliminate body contact with the water and at least 12 square inches of international orange (a baseball cap works) twelve inches above the water. In addition, tubers must stay within 150 feet of shore, but may cross the lake at the east buoy line. They also must carry a whistle or air horn to warn boats.

The lake's rental boats are available on a first-come, first-served basis. Boat rentals are $8.00 per day, $6.00 per half day. Rental boats with 3-horsepower motors are $18.00 per day, $14.00 per half day. The fee for launching your own boat is $4.00. Boats shorter than 10 feet and longer than 20 feet are prohibited, and the lake has a 5-mile-per-hour speed limit, but it also has no personal watercraft or water skiers to disturb the fishing. For more information, contact the lake ranger's office at (760) 738-4346. Bob's Bait and Tackle in Escondido has some fishing information; phone (760) 741-1570.

Two resorts near the lake are Lake Wohlford Resort, (760) 749-2755, on the north shore, and Oakvale Park, (760) 749-2895, on the south. Both have full-hookup sites, plus Oakvale has some regular campsites. Escondido is a good-sized town and has all services, except for fly shops. Lake Dixon, also operated by the city, is just a few miles away, and Lake Hodges, one of the famed San Diego city lakes, is in the south end of Escondido. Vacationing anglers can bring the family to see the San Diego Wild Animal Park in Escondido while the rest of the family fishes.

DIXON LAKE AND LAKE POWAY

These two small lakes in San Diego County don't merit the full treatment I've given to the other angling possibilities above, but they deserve mention for one head-turning reason. Each holds one of the seven International Game Fish Association fly-rod line-class records for largemouth bass. Both records were set by the same angler, Dennis Ditmars. His record for Dixon is a 10-pound, 2-ounce largemouth on a 6-pound tippet, and the Poway fish weighed 9 pounds, 5 ounces taken on a substantial 20-pound tippet.

Poway and Dixon Lakes are not large (Dixon is 70 acres, Poway is 60), but they have bass with Florida genes, and they get hatchery trout during the cold months. Each has produced some huge bass, not just for Dennis Ditmars, but also for other fishermen, and I think any fly angler who wants to be a record holder and has a bit of persistence could have a chance of doing so here. As a bonus, because they are not better known, fishing can be quite pleasant. Ditmars said the main reason he fished for bass in these lakes was the peace and quiet. Other San Diego County waters can have a lot of traffic.

Both lakes remind me of the 7-acre pond near Santa Rosa in Northern California. where conventional-tackle angler Paul Duclos caught what may have been a new world-record bass in 1997. This big fish, estimated to weigh some 24 pounds, was released alive and could not be examined or properly weighed to make any record official. Like that little pond, both Dixon and Poway have Florida-strain largemouths and get regular plants of trout during the winter.

Neither lake permits wading or float-tube fishing, and both prohibit private boats. Rental boats are available, and you can bring an electric motor to get you around. For more information on these small but interesting waters, call (760) 741-4680 for Dixon Lake and (760) 679-5466 for Poway.

INFORMATION SOURCES

For an area the size of Southern California, the dearth of angling information is startling. Many fly anglers simply don't realize the range of fishing opportunities available within an hour or two's drive of even the most urban parts of the Los Angeles metropolitan area.

Lack of information leads to ignorance. Moreover, things change rapidly in Southern California, especially information on contacts. Trying to keep track of telephone numbers and especially area codes and web-site URLs is almost a full-time job.

The guides, shops, fishing clubs, and various state and federal agencies listed here, however, should help you make the fullest use of this guidebook. And with luck, maybe we'll meet on one of the local waters. I'd very much like to trade fish stories with you.

FLY SHOPS AND GUIDES

Conway Bowman
Bowman Bluewater Guide Service
(619) 697-4997
A San Diego area saltwater guide, Bowman also guides fly anglers on local bass lakes and trout streams.

Fisherman's Spot!
14423 Burbank Boulevard, Van Nuys, CA 91401
(818) 785-7306

High Sierra Flyfisher
337 W. Ridgecrest Boulevard, Ridgecrest, CA 93555
(760) 375-5810

Bob Marriott's Flyfishing Store
2700 W. Orangethorpe Avenue, Fullerton, CA 92833
(714) 525-1827; www.bobmarriotts.com

San Diego Fly Shop
4401 Twain Avenue, Suite #6, San Diego, CA 92120
(619) 283-3445, (800) 363-FISH
Offers guide service for both freshwater and saltwater fishing.

Mike Scott's Hackle, Tackle, and Flies
2324 N. Batavia Street, Suite 116, Orange, CA 92665
(714) 998-9400

Bob Slamal
Riverside Ski and Sport
6744 Brockton Avenue, Riverside, CA 92506
(909) 784-0205
Slamal guides for bass and stripers on local waters.

Stroud Tackle
1457 Morena Boulevard, San Diego, CA
(619) 276-4822

Randy Weir
Tight Lines Guide Service
9992 Cheyenne Circle, Ventura, CA 93004
(805) 659-4462
Guides on Sespe Creek and local Ventura County waters.

FLY FISHING CLUBS, FEDERATION OF FLY FISHERS SOUTHWEST COUNCIL

Aguabonita Fly Fishers
P.O. Box 2059, Ridgecrest, CA 93556

Antelope Valley Fly Rodders
P.O. Box 3231, Quartz Hill, CA 93586

Arroyo Fly Fishers
c/o Arroyo High School, 4291 N. Cedar Avenue, El Monte, CA 91732

Conejo Valley Fly Fishers
3166 E. Thousand Oaks Boulevard, Thousand Oaks, CA 91362

Deep Creek Fly Fishers
P.O. Box 7735, Redlands, CA 92375-0735

Downey Fly Fishers
P.O. Box 516, Downey, CA 90241

Fly Fishers Club of Orange County
P.O. Box 23005, Santa Ana, CA 92711-3005

Inland Flyfishing Club
P.O. Box 3662, Cerritos, CA 90703

Kaweah Fly Fishers
P.O. Box 3704, Visalia, CA 93230

Kern River Fly Fishers
P.O. Box 686, Bakersfield, CA 90703

Las Vegas Fly Fishing Club
P.O. Box 27958, Las Vegas, NV 89112

Long Beach Casting Club
P.O. Box 90035, Long Beach, CA 90809

Pasadena Casting Club
P.O. Box 6, Pasadena, CA 91102

Salt Water Fly Rodders, Pacific No. 1
P.O. Box 245, Montrose, CA 91020

San Diego Fly Fishers
1457 Morena Boulevard, San Diego, CA 92110

San Gabriel Valley Fly Fishers
321 So. Charvers Avenue, West Coven, CA 91791

Santa Barbara Fly Fishers
P.O. Box 24012, Santa Barbara, CA 93121-4012

Sespe Fly Fishers
P.O. Box 5127, Ventura, CA 93003

Sierra Pacific Fly Fishers
P.O. Box 8403, Van Nuys, CA

Southbay Fly Fishers
P.O. Box 5298, Playa Del Rey, CA 90296

Streamborn Fly Fishing Club
P.O. Box 8284, Rowland Heights, CA 91748

Wilderness Fly Fishers
P.O. Box 3358, Santa Monica, CA 90408-3358

EDUCATION AND CONSERVATION GROUPS

California Trout
870 Market Street, #859, San Francisco, CA 94102
(415) 392-8895

California Sportfishing Protection Alliance
P.O. Box 357, Quincy, CA 95951
(530) 836-1115

Trout Unlimited of California
828 San Pablo Ave.,#208, Albany, CA 94709
(510) 528-4772

Fisheries Resource Volunteer Corps
P.O. Box 6551, San Pedro, CA 90734
(714) 284-8844
A small group of interested anglers who work with the U.S. Forest Service to monitor and patrol Southern California trout streams.

BOOKS, MAGAZINES, MAPS, AND WEB SITES

In addition to this guide, there are a number of good books, magazines, maps, and Web sites that offer information on every aspect of angling in Southern California.

Bass Fishing in California: Secrets of the Western Pros
by Ron Kovach. Marketscope Books, 119 Richard, Aptos, CA 95003
Don't be put off by the title. This is in fact a book for conventional-tackle bass anglers, but it also contains quite a bit of useful information for warmwater fly anglers in the Southland.

Boating Trail Guide to the Colorado River
California Department of Boating and Waterways
1629 S. Street, Sacramento, CA 95814
This small booklet of maps is designed for canoe and raft enthusiasts, but has a considerable amount of information for anglers. The maps include all landings and campgrounds.

California Fly Fisher
P.O. Box 8535, Truckee, CA 96162
Published six times per year, it's the only magazine dedicated to fly fishing in the Golden State, and provides good coverage of Southern California angling opportunities.

California Game & Fish
Game & Fish Publications Inc., P.O. Box 741,
Marietta, GA 30061
Published twelve times per year, California Game & Fish is a general outdoor publication, but has monthly articles on fishing throughout the state.

California Road & Recreation Atlas
Benchmark Maps, 30 S. La Patera Lane, Unit #5, Santa Barbara, CA 93177
(805) 692-6777
www.maps-eureka.com
A new state atlas of high quality, available in most book, map, and office supply stores.

Fish-n-Map Co.
8535 W. 79th Avenue, Arvada, CO 80005
(303) 421-5994
www.fishnmap.com
Fine lake topographic maps for popular waters in several Western states. These usually have two or more lakes per map. Fish-n-Map has both Southern California and Northern California maps. The maps are printed on waterproof, tear-resistant plastic paper. They are sold at many fishing shops and marinas.

FHS Lake Maps
1-800-ALL-MAPS
FHS (Fishing Hot Spots) maps cover much of the United States. For California lakes, there are twelve maps at present, which cover waters in both Northern and Southern California.

Lake Recreation in Southern California for Weekenders
by Herschell Whitmer and Scott Whitmer. Herschell Whitmer Associates, P.O. Box 7261, Long Beach, CA 90807
A concise guidebook to still waters in Southern California. Very handy. Includes information on day use fees, camping, fishing and boating, and a number of other topics.

The Old Pro Fish Finder Maps
P.O. Box 681, Baldwin Park, CA 91706
A good selection of California lake maps showing structure. Sold in bass pro shops and marinas.

Recreation Lakes of California
D. J. Dirksen. Recreation Sales Publishing, P.O. Box 1028, Aptos, CA 95001
Covers the whole state with slightly less detail for each lake covered than Lake Recreation in Southern California for Weekenders, but a very handy book for your library,

Reel Maps
2532 Lincoln Boulevard, #91, Venice, CA 90291
(310) 822-1827
A series of hand-painted stream maps.

Southern & Central California Atlas & Gazetteer
DeLorme Mapping Co., P.O. Box 298, Freeport, MA 04032
(207) 865-4171
An excellent state atlas in two parts: Northern and Southern-Central California. Available in book, map, and office supply stores and in many fly shops.

GENERAL-INFORMATION WEB SITES

I've included only a few prime Web sites, most of which show links to just about every other site of interest within California and more specifically within the area covered by this guidebook. Because people and organizations change Internet service providers and URL addresses frequently, use a search engine to find the listed site if the URL is out of date.

California Department of Fish and Game
www.dfg.ca.gov.
Look for the new wild-trout Web site via this one.

California Trout
www.caltrout.org

Federation of Fly Fishers
www.fedflyfishers.org/index2.html

Federation of Fly Fishers, Southwest Council
www.calflytech.com/swcfff/

Fly Fish Arizona
www.azlink.com/~jshannon/
Has links to several Southern California club sites and other information of interest to Southern California fly fishers.

Fly Fisherman Magazine Virtual Fly Shop
www.flyshop.com

Turner's Outdoorsman
www.turners.com
A chain of sporting-goods stores. These are not fly shops, but their Web site has an excellent fishing report by Jim Matthews, of Outdoor News Service, plus many other items of interest.

DEPARTMENT OF FISH AND GAME, REGIONS 5 AND 6, SOUTHERN CALIFORNIA

Region 5 Main Office, 330 Golden Shore, Suite 50, Long Beach, CA 90802, (562) 590-5132.
(Inland Fisheries Office, (562) 590-5151.)

Region 6 Main Office
4775 Bird Farm Road
Chino, CA 91709, (909) 597-0067

Eastern Sierra Office, 407 West Line Street, Bishop, CA 93514, (760) 872-1171.

San Diego Area Office, 4949 Viewridge Avenue, San Diego, CA 92123, (619) 467-4201.
Trout plants recording, (562) 590-5020.

NATIONAL FOREST OFFICES IN SOUTHERN CALIFORNIA

Anglers interested in the many streams within national forest areas can contact each for maps. These are normally very good, although significant Forest Service Route closures frequently are not shown because the maps are updated only every few years. One nice feature is the later versions show the USGS topographic quads that cover the same area. You can order these quads from the U.S. Geological Survey, Box 25286, Federal Center, Denver, CO 80225. Most backpacking and sporting-goods stores sell topo maps for the area where they are located.

Angeles National Forest
701 N. Santa Anita Avenue, Arcadia, CA 91006
(626) 574-1613

Mount Baldy District Office, Angeles National Forest
10 N. Wabash Avenue, Glendora, CA 91740
(626) 335-1251

Cleveland National Forest
10845 Rancho Bernardo, Suite 200, San Diego, CA 92127
(619) 673-6180

Los Padres National Forest
6144 Calle Real, Goleta, CA 93117
(626) 683-6711

San Bernardino National Forest
1824 Commercenter Circle, San Bernardino, CA 92408
(909) 383-5588